200 healthy feasts

hamlyn | all colour cookbook

200 healthy feasts

Jo McAuley

An Hachette UK company
www.hachette.co.uk

First published in Great Britain in 2011 by Hamlyn,
a division of Octopus Publishing Group Ltd
Endeavour House, 189 Shaftesbury Avenue
London WC2H 8JY
www.octopusbooks.co.uk

Copyright © Octopus Publishing Group Ltd 2011

Some of the recipes in this book have previously appeared in
other books published by Hamlyn.

ISBN: 978-0-600-62355-7

A CIP catalogue record for this book is available from the
British Library

Printed and bound in China

1 2 3 4 5 6 7 8 9 10

Both metric and imperial measurements have been given
in all recipes. Use one set of measurements only, and not a
mixture of both.

Standard level spoon measurements are used in all recipes.
1 tablespoon = one 15 ml spoon
1 teaspoon = one 5 ml spoon

Ovens should be preheated to the specified temperature
– if using a fan-assisted oven, follow the manufacturer's
instructions for adjusting the time and the temperature.

The Department of Health advises that eggs should not be
consumed raw. This book contains some dishes made with
raw or lightly cooked eggs. It is prudent for vulnerable people,
such as pregnant and nursing mothers, invalids, the elderly,
babies and young children to avoid uncooked or lightly
cooked dishes made with eggs. Once prepared, these dishes
should be kept refrigerated and used promptly.

This book includes dishes made with nuts and nut derivatives.
It is advisable for those with known allergic reactions to
nuts and nut derivatives and those who may be potentially
vulnerable to these allergies to avoid dishes made with nuts
and nut oils. It is also prudent to check the labels of
pre-prepared ingredients for the possible inclusion
of nut derivatives.

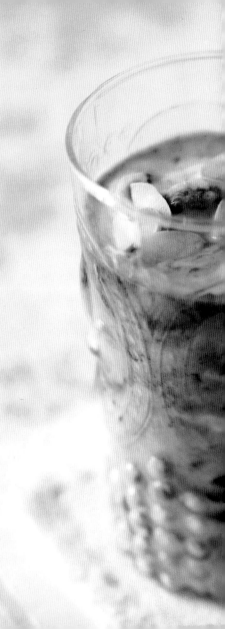

contents

introduction

introduction

If your aim is to eat healthily, but you dread feeling hungry and lacking in energy, then this is the book for you – it is full of delicious, substantial and nutritious recipes designed to satisfy even the biggest appetites and keep you going until the next meal. This book will show you that 'healthy' doesn't have to mean 'boring'. The great flavours, appearance and aromas from the recipes it contains will appeal to all your senses, and the energy-boosting ingredients used will help to reduce any craving and your desire to snack while keeping energy levels high. By following the recipes in this book, you will find it easier and

more enjoyable to eat a healthy, well-balanced diet without the feeling that you are being denied all the 'good stuff', and this could change the way you eat forever.

reasons to eat healthily

There are so many reasons to keep your body healthy, and the way you eat often has a direct influence on the way you feel. Eating a well-balanced diet with plenty of the essential proteins, vitamins, nutrients, carbohydrates and essential fats is very important in maintaining good health. It can help control cholesterol, as well going a long way towards avoiding constipation, bad skin and poor hair condition.

It has also been proven that a healthy diet can help us to avoid serious conditions such as coronary heart disease, strokes and even some cancers. For example, a diet rich in fibre can reduce the risk of bowel cancer.

The path to general well-being through the aid of a healthy diet doesn't usually have to mean a complete overhaul in the way that you eat. More often, it is just a few subtle changes in the way that you think and cook that will leave you reaping the rewards in both the short and long term.

'5 a day'

With the enormous choice and variety available to us today, it's easier than you might think for you and your family to get all of the recommended five portions of fruit

and vegetables a day. Almost all fruit and vegetables, and even beans and pulses, count towards one of your '5 a day', whether they come fresh, frozen, dried or canned.

One adult-sized portion of fruit or vegetable weighs approximately 80 g (just over 3 oz), or roughly the amount that will fit into the palm of your hand. Even a glass of fruit juice or a smoothie counts, although it's best not to drink more than one of these each day as the sugars they contain can do damage to your teeth in the long term.

Eating five portions of fruit and vegetables each day really will improve your health. Consuming your '5 a day' can be achieved on any budget, no matter how busy your lifestyle. It just takes a little planning and effort.

the GI

GI stands for the Glycaemic Index. Foods containing carbohydrates have an effect on blood sugar levels and can be distinguished by either a high- or low-level GI.

Foods with a high GI value release sugar into the bloodstream quickly, giving you that familiar 'sugar rush'. This rise in blood sugar, however, doesn't last very long and quickly leaves you feeling tired, hungry and low in energy.

Foods with a low GI value, however, release sugar into the bloodstream slowly, supplying a slow, steady source of energy. This leaves you feeling satisfied for a longer period of

time, which in turn results in less snacking throughout the day.

The recipes in this book tend to include lots of GI foods, such as wholewheat pasta, beans, pulses, lentils, yogurt, fruits and vegetables.

starchy foods

Starchy foods are an important part of a healthy diet. They include foods such as pasta, rice, cereals and bread and are a vital part of any meal, as they provide a great source of energy and essential nutrients. Try to choose wholegrain and wholemeal varieties of starchy foods, such as wholewheat pasta and couscous, brown rice and wholemeal bread, as they have a low GI value and will keep you feeling satisfied for longer.

fish

Eating plenty of fish will help ensure that your body is getting lots of important vitamins and minerals. We are recommended to eat a minimum of two portions of fish a week, of which at least one should be from an oily fish, which is high in omega-3 fats. Oily fish include tuna, salmon, mackerel, herring and sardines. It's a good idea to try steaming or poaching your fish, in order to retain as many nutrients as possible.

fats

Not all fats are bad. Some are essential when eating a healthy, balanced diet. Our bodies cannot provide us with all the essential fatty

acids that we need to stay healthy, so it is important to include them in our diets. Extra virgin olive and rapeseed oils are a great source of unsaturated fats, which are also found naturally in oily fish, nuts and seeds. It is recommended to avoid eating too many saturated fats, as there are fears that they could increase the risk of high cholesterol and coronary heart disease.

salt and sugar

Salt and sugar are two foods that it is advisable to cut back on. To reduce the risk of getting high blood pressure, and therefore reduce the risk of strokes and heart disease, it is important not to eat too much salt. Try flavouring food with herbs, spices and lemon juice, and always taste your food before automatically adding salt.

Added sugar is an ingredient that our bodies can do without. Try instead to get sweetness from foods that have naturally occurring sugars in them, such as fruit, and if you do need to add sugar, try to use the least refined sorts possible. Palm sugar and agave nectar are less processed alternatives.

fibre

Fibre is a vital part of a healthy diet if you want to avoid constipation, bowel cancer and various other digestive problems. As well the more obvious foods, such as breads, pasta, rice and potatoes, fruit and vegetables also have lots of natural dietary fibre. To boost your

intake, try adding a portion of raw vegetable salad or a handful of crushed whole nuts to your meal.

protein and dairy

Protein is essential for the repair and growth of our bodies. As well as lean meat and fish, try to include eggs, beans and pulses in your diet – all are great sources of protein. Dairy produce is also a good source of protein as well as calcium, essential for keeping our bones healthy. Try drinking skimmed or semi-skimmed milk, which contains the same amount of calcium as full-fat milk, but less saturated fats.

some healthy cooking methods

- Steaming is a gentle way to cook vegetables, fish and lean cuts of meat, ensuring a great texture while locking the nutrients in. Whether you want to cook with a fancy electric steamer, a simple steamer basket or an Asian-style bamboo steamer, this is one of the healthiest forms of cooking.

- Poaching in liquid is also a great way of cooking fish and meat while keeping it tender and moist. It's a really versatile way of cooking, and the combinations of flavours you can use when poaching are endless.

- Grilling or griddling is a healthy form of cooking fattier cuts of meat, as it allows the fat to melt away from the meat and run off, leaving you with a delicious grilled taste, but without the excess fat. Using a heavy, ridged griddle pan is also a great way to cook

vegetables, such as strips of aubergine and courgette, without having to add extra oil while cooking.

- Stir-frying is a really healthy way of cooking food quickly while retaining texture, taste and nutrients. You only need to use small amounts of oil in a well-seasoned wok or large frying pan over a very high heat. Stir-frying is the ultimate healthy way of cooking 'fast food'.

- Slow cooking, either in a slow cooker designed especially for the purpose, or in a casserole in the oven or on the hob, is a perfect way of cooking some of the tougher cuts of meat, without compromising on taste. The long, slow, gentle cooking allows the flavours to really develop while giving the meat really drop-off-the-bone tenderness. You can then skim any excess fat from the top of the dish when it has finished cooking.

tips for healthy eating

- Do invest in a really good, nonstick frying pan. It will drastically reduce the amount of oil you will need to cook with.

- Don't skip breakfast! Eating breakfast in the morning is a chance to refuel your body and get your metabolism going. This is essential if you want to keep your energy levels high while avoiding the trap of snacking throughout the morning.

- Do try using an olive oil spray to grease your pans and tins. It is an easier way to control how much oil you use, both for cooking and on salads.

- Don't do diets that are going to make your weight 'yo-yo'. Rapid weight loss can be more damaging to your health, and weight is much more likely to go back on once the diet is finished. It is much healthier for both body and mind to make some simple changes to the way that you cook and eat. If you eat healthily and exercise sensibly, you will be much more likely to reach your goal weight and stick to it.

- Do replace high sugar or salty snacks with more natural alternatives. Eaten in moderation, nuts, seeds and dried fruits are much healthier snacks and likely to satisfy any cravings. Try cutting up raw vegetables into batons and serving with fat-free Greek yogurt mixed with fresh herbs and lemon juice for a totally guilt-free evening snack.

- Don't over-season your food with salt or sugar during cooking; if you do, it cannot be removed. Instead, season lightly during the cooking process and encourage your family to add a squeeze of lemon juice or some extra spices to replace any extra salt, which is bad for your health in large quantities.

- Do exercise! We are recommended to do at least 30 minutes of exercise each day in order to stay fit and healthy. Low-impact activities, such as walking, yoga, aerobics and swimming, are all great ways to introduce a little exercise into your life without risking damage to joints.

breakfast &
brunch

porridge with prune compote

Serves 4–8
Preparation time **5 minutes**
Cooking time **about**
  20 minutes

1 litre (1¾ pints) **skimmed** or
  semi-skimmed milk
500 ml (17 fl oz) **water**
1 teaspoon **vanilla extract**
pinch of **ground cinnamon**
pinch of **salt**
200 g (7 oz) **porridge oats**
3 tablespoons **flaked**
  almonds, toasted

Compote
250 g (8 oz) **ready-to-eat**
  dried Agen prunes
125 ml (4 fl oz) **apple juice**
1 small **cinnamon stick**
1 **clove**
1 tablespoon **mild agave**
  nectar or **runny honey**
1 unpeeled **orange** quarter

Place all the compote ingredients in a small saucepan over a medium heat. Simmer gently for 10–12 minutes or until softened and slightly sticky. Leave to cool. (The compote can be prepared in advance and chilled.)

Put the milk, measurement water, vanilla extract, cinnamon and salt in a large saucepan over a medium heat and bring slowly to the boil. Stir in the oats, then reduce the heat and simmer gently, stirring occasionally, for 8–10 minutes until creamy and tender.

Spoon the porridge into bowls, scatter with the almonds and serve with the prune compote.

For sweet quinoa porridge with banana & dates, put 250 g (8 oz) quinoa in a saucepan with the milk, agave nectar or honey and 2–3 cardamom pods. Simmer gently for 12–15 minutes or until the quinoa is cooked and the desired consistency is reached. Serve in bowls topped with dollops of fat-free natural yogurt, 100 g (3½ oz) chopped dates and freshly sliced banana.

bacon & mushroom frittata

Serves **4**

Preparation time **5 minutes**

Cooking time **25–30 minutes**

8 **portabella** or **flat chestnut
mushrooms**, about 500 g
(1 lb) in total

1 **garlic clove**, finely chopped
(optional)

olive oil spray

4 lean **smoked back bacon
rashers**

6 large **eggs**

1 tablespoon **chopped chives**,
plus extra to garnish

1 tablespoon **wholegrain
mustard**

knob of **butter**

4 large slices of **sourdough
bread**

salt and **pepper**

Put the mushrooms on a foil-lined baking sheet and
scatter over the garlic, if using. Spray with a little olive oil,
season with salt and pepper and place in a preheated
oven, 180°C (350°F), Gas Mark 4, for 18–20 minutes or
until softened. Leave until cool enough to handle.

Meanwhile, lay the bacon rashers on a foil-lined grill
pan and cook under a preheated medium-hot grill for
5–6 minutes, turning once or until slightly crispy. Cool
slightly, then slice thickly.

Put the eggs, chives and mustard in a bowl, beat
together lightly and season with pepper.

Heat a large, nonstick frying pan with an ovenproof
handle, add the butter and melt until beginning to froth.
Pour in the egg mixture and cook for 1–2 minutes,
then add the bacon and whole mushrooms, stalk side
up. Cook for a further 2–3 minutes or until almost set.
Place the pan under a preheated hot grill and cook the
frittata for 2–3 minutes until set, then cool slightly.

Toast the bread and arrange on serving plates. Cut
the frittata into wedges and serve on the toasted
sourdough, garnished with chives.

For mushroom & bacon quiche, roll out 375 g
(12 oz) ready-made, wholemeal shortcrust pastry to
fit a lightly greased 23 cm (9 inch) quiche tin and
bake blind (i.e. bake the empty case without filling) in
the preheated oven for 12–15 minutes or until lightly
golden. Cook the mushrooms and bacon as above and
scatter over the pastry shell. Fill with the beaten egg
mixture and return to the oven for 25–30 minutes or
until risen and cooked.

granola with peaches & yogurt

Serves **4**
Preparation time **15 minutes**,
  plus cooling
Cooking time **45 minutes**

200 g (7 oz) **rolled oats**
50 g (2 oz) **wheatgerm**
50 g (2 oz) **sunflower seeds**
25 g (1 oz) **sesame seeds** or
  linseeds
50 g (2 oz) **pumpkin seeds**
50 g (2 oz) **whole blanched
  almonds**
50 g (2 oz) **hazelnuts**
½ teaspoon **ground
  cinnamon**
½ teaspoon **ground mixed
  spice**
¼ teaspoon **salt**
100 ml (3½ fl oz) **maple syrup**
1 tablespoon **molasses** or
  treacle
2 tablespoons **vegetable** or
  rapeseed oil
75 g (3 oz) **ready-to-eat dried
  apricots**, chopped
50 g (2 oz) **dried cranberries**
50 g (2 oz) **golden raisins**
350 g (11½ oz) **fat-free
  Greek yogurt**
2 **peaches**, stoned and sliced

Mix together the cereals, seeds, nuts, spices and salt in a large bowl.

Heat the maple syrup, molasses or treacle, oil and 2 tablespoons water in a small saucepan, then pour over the dry ingredients. Stir until thoroughly combined.

Tip the mixture on to a large, lightly oiled baking sheet, then press down firmly to make clumps. Place in a preheated oven, 140°C (275°F), Gas Mark 1, for about 30 minutes. Add the dried fruits and stir gently to combine. Return to the oven for a further 15 minutes or until evenly crisp and golden brown.

Leave to cool on the baking sheet (it will continue to crisp up as it cools), then store in an airtight container for up to 1 week. To serve, spoon into serving bowls and top with the yogurt and peaches.

For no-sugar toasted muesli, put the rolled oats, wheatgerm, sunflower seeds and chopped nuts in a large, nonstick frying pan in batches and dry-fry. Stir in the cinnamon and mixed spice and leave to cool completely before storing in an airtight container. To serve, spoon into bowls and add dried or fresh fruit, if liked.

herby smoked salmon omelettes

Serves **4**
Preparation time **10 minutes**
Cooking time **about
  15 minutes**

8 **large eggs**
2 **spring onions**, thinly sliced
2 tablespoons **chopped
  chives**
2 tablespoons **chopped
  chervil**
50 g (2 oz) **butter**
4 thin slices of **smoked
  salmon**, cut into thin strips,
  or 125 g (4 oz) **smoked
  salmon trimmings**
pepper

Put the eggs, spring onions and herbs in a bowl, beat together lightly and season with pepper.

Heat a medium-sized frying pan over a medium-low heat, add a quarter of the butter and melt until beginning to froth. Pour in a quarter of the egg mixture and swirl to cover the base of the pan. Stir gently for 2–3 minutes or until almost set.

Sprinkle over a quarter of the smoked salmon strips and cook for a further 30 seconds or until just set. Fold over and slide on to a serving plate. Repeat to make 3 more omelettes. Serve each omelette immediately with baby leaf and herb salad.

For smoked ham & tomato omelette, make as above, adding 8–12 quartered cherry tomatoes to the egg mixture. Replace the smoked salmon with 4 thin slices of smoked ham, cut into strips.

fruity summer smoothie

Makes **4 x 300 ml (½ pint) glasses**
Preparation time **2 minutes**

2 **peaches**, halved, pitted and chopped
300 g (10 oz) **strawberries**
300 g (10 oz) **raspberries**
400 ml (14 fl oz) **skimmed** or **semi-skimmed milk**
ice cubes

Put the peach in a blender or food processor with the strawberries and raspberries and blend to a smooth purée, scraping the mixture down from the sides of the bowl if necessary.

Add the milk and blend the ingredients again until the mixture is smooth and frothy. Pour the milkshake over the ice cubes in tall glasses.

For soya milk & mango shake, replace the peach, strawberries and raspberries with 2 large ripe mangoes and the juice of 2 oranges. Purée as above, then pour in 400 ml (14 fl oz) soya milk, blend and serve over ice cubes as above.

home-baked seeded rolls

Makes **8 rolls**

Preparation time **25 minutes**,
plus proving

Cooking time **12–15 minutes**

500 g (1 lb) **strong plain** or
wholegrain bread flour

50 g (2 oz) **mixed seeds**

1 teaspoon **fast-action dried
yeast**

1 teaspoon **sugar**

1 teaspoon **salt**

275 ml (9 fl oz) **hand-hot
water**

1 tablespoon **melted butter**

Put the flour, seeds and yeast in a large bowl, then stir
in the sugar and salt. Pour in the measurement water
and butter and mix to a dough. Turn the dough out on a
lightly floured surface and knead for 5–10 minutes or
until smooth and elastic.

Place in a lightly oiled bowl, cover with a clean, slightly
damp tea towel and leave in a warm place to rise for
at least 1 hour or until doubled in size. Alternatively,
make the dough in a bread machine according to the
manufacturer's instructions.

Push the dough back down and then divide into 8 balls.
Knead each piece until smooth and round, then place
evenly spaced on a large, lightly greased baking sheet.
Cut a deep cross in each one, cover again with the
damp tea towel and leave in a warm place to rise for
1 hour or until doubled in size.

Bake the rolls in a preheated oven, 200°C (400°F),
Gas Mark 6, for 12–15 minutes or until golden and
crusty and the rolls sound hollow when tapped on the
underside. Cool slightly on a wire rack, pulling apart if
they have spread during rising or cooking. Serve warm,
split in half, with a bowl of thick-cut orange marmalade
and a glass of freshly squeezed fruit juice, if liked.

For mixed seed loaf, make the dough as above but
form into 1 large, round loaf. Leave to rise until doubled
in size and then cook in the oven for 30 minutes or until
golden and crusty and the loaf sounds hollow when
tapped on the underside. Cool on a wire rack. Cut into
slices and serve warm or toasted.

banana muffins

Makes **12**
Preparation time **10 minutes**
Cooking time **20–22 minutes**

200 g (7 oz) **unbleached plain flour**
35 g (1½ oz) **bran**
75 g (3 oz) **soft dark brown sugar**
1 teaspoon **baking powder**
¾ teaspoon **bicarbonate of soda**
½ teaspoon **ground mixed spice** (optional)
200 ml (7 fl oz) **buttermilk**
2½ tablespoons **groundnut oil**
2 **large eggs**, beaten
1 teaspoon **vanilla extract**
2 small, **very ripe bananas**, peeled and mashed

Mix together the dry ingredients in a large bowl. Stir together the remaining ingredients in a separate bowl, then pour the wet ingredients on to the dry mixture and stir with a large metal spoon until just combined.

Spoon the mixture into a lightly greased large, 12-hole nonstick muffin tray, or alternatively, a 6-hole tray, and bake in a preheated oven, 180°C (350°F), Gas Mark 4, for 20–22 minutes or until risen and golden and a skewer inserted into the centres comes out clean.

Transfer to a wire rack to cool slightly. Serve the still-warm muffins with glasses of freshly squeezed fruit juice, if liked.

For banana, blueberry & wheatgerm muffins, make as above, replacing 1 of the bananas with 125 g (4 oz) blueberries, the bran with 35 g (1½ oz) wheatgerm and the mixed spice with ½ teaspoon ground cinnamon.

poached eggs & spinach

Serves **4**
Preparation time **5 minutes**
Cooking time **8–10 minutes**

4 strips of **cherry tomatoes**
 on the vine, about
 6 tomatoes on each
2 tablespoons **balsamic syrup**
 or **glaze**
1 small bunch of **basil**, leaves
 removed
1 tablespoon **distilled vinegar**
4 large **eggs**
4 thick slices of **wholemeal
 bread**
reduced-fat butter, to spread
 (optional)
100 g (3½ oz) **baby leaf
 spinach**
salt and **pepper**

Lay the cherry tomato vines in an ovenproof dish, drizzle with the balsamic syrup or glaze, scatter with the basil leaves and season with salt and pepper. Place in a preheated oven, 180°C (350°F), Gas Mark 4, for 8–10 minutes or until the tomatoes begin to collapse.

Meanwhile, bring a large saucepan of water to a gentle simmer, add the vinegar and stir with a large spoon to create a swirl. Carefully break 2 eggs into the water and cook for 3 minutes. Remove with a slotted spoon and keep warm. Repeat with the remaining eggs.

Toast the wholemeal bread and butter lightly, if liked.

Heap the spinach on to serving plates and top each plate with a poached egg. Arrange the vine tomatoes on the plates, drizzled with any cooking juices. Serve immediately with the wholemeal toast, cut into fingers.

For spinach, egg & cress salad, gently lower the unshelled eggs into a saucepan of simmering water. Cook for 7–8 minutes, then cool quickly under running cold water. Shell the eggs and slice thickly. Arrange the egg slices over the spinach leaves and halved cherry tomatoes. Scatter with 20 g (¾ oz) salad cress and serve with a little olive oil and balsamic syrup.

starters & light bites

carrot & cashew nut salad

Serves **4**

Preparation time **10 minutes**

Cooking time **6–10 minutes**

75 g (3 oz) **unsalted cashew nuts**

2 tablespoons **black mustard seeds**

500 g (1 lb) **carrots**, peeled and coarsely grated

1 **red pepper**, cored, deseeded and thinly sliced

3 tablespoons chopped **chervil**

2 **spring onions**, finely sliced

Dressing

2 tablespoons **avocado oil**

2 tablespoons **raspberry vinegar**

1 tablespoon **wholegrain mustard**

pinch of **sugar**

salt and **pepper**

Heat a nonstick frying pan over a medium-low heat and dry-fry the cashew nuts for 5–8 minutes, stirring frequently, or until golden brown and toasted. Tip on to a small plate and leave to cool. Add the mustard seeds to the pan and dry-fry for 1–2 minutes or until they start to pop.

Mix together the mustard seeds, carrots, red pepper, chervil and spring onions in a large bowl.

Whisk together all the dressing ingredients in a small bowl, then pour on to the grated carrot salad. Mix thoroughly to coat and heap into serving bowls.

Chop the cashew nuts coarsely and scatter over the salad. Serve immediately.

For carrot & celeriac coleslaw, mix together 300 g (10 oz) grated carrot and 200 g (7 oz) coarsely grated celeriac with the mustard seeds, chervil, spring onions and dressing, omitting the red pepper. Replace the cashew nuts with 75 g (3 oz) chopped walnuts and serve as above.

fig, bean & toasted pecan salad

Serves **4**
Preparation time **5 minutes**,
  plus cooling
Cooking time **5–6 minutes**

100 g (3½ oz) **pecan nuts**
200 g (7 oz) **green beans**,
  trimmed
4 **fresh figs**, cut into quarters
100 g (3½ oz) **rocket leaves**
small handful of **mint leaves**
50 g (2 oz) **Parmesan** or
  pecorino cheese

Dressing
3 tablespoons **walnut oil**
2 teaspoons **sherry vinegar**
1 teaspoon **vincotto**
salt and **pepper**

Heat a heavy-based frying pan over a medium heat,
add the pecan nuts and dry-fry, stirring frequently, for
3–4 minutes or until browned. Tip on to a small plate
and leave to cool.

Cook the beans in a saucepan of lightly salted boiling
water for 2 minutes. Drain, refresh under running cold
water and pat dry with kitchen paper. Put the beans in a
bowl with the figs, pecan nuts, rocket and mint.

Whisk together all the dressing ingredients in a small
bowl and season with salt and paper. If you can't find
vincotto, use balsamic vinegar as an alternative. Pour
over the salad and toss well. Shave over the Parmesan
or pecorino and serve.

For mixed bean salad, combine 200 g (7 oz) cooked
trimmed green beans with 2 x 400 g (13 oz) cans
drained mixed beans, 4 finely chopped spring onions,
1 crushed garlic clove and 4 tablespoons chopped
mixed herbs, then dress with 4 tablespoons olive
oil, juice of ½ lemon, a pinch of caster sugar and salt
and pepper.

watermelon, feta & herb salad

Serves **4**
Preparation time **15 minutes**

¼ **watermelon**, about 800 g
  (1¾ lb 10 oz) in total, peeled
  and cut into large chunks
1 small bunch of **parsley**, finely
  chopped
1 small bunch of **mint**, finely
  chopped
1 small bunch of **coriander**,
  finely chopped
200 g (7 oz) **reduced-fat feta
  cheese**, cubed
16 pitted **Greek olives**
1 tablespoon **red jalapeño
  peppers in brine**, drained
  and finely chopped
juice of 1 **lime**, plus extra
  wedges, to serve
small handful of **alfalfa** or
  radish shoots, to garnish

Put the watermelon, herbs, feta, olives and jalapeño peppers in a large bowl and toss together.

Spoon into serving dishes and pour over the lime juice. Garnish with the alfalfa or radish shoots and serve with lime wedges and grissini breadsticks, if liked.

For watermelon fruit salad, mix together the watermelon and chopped mint with 2 peeled, sliced kiwi fruit, 200 g (7 oz) halved red grapes, 2 small, peeled, cored and thinly sliced apples and 200 g (7 oz) pitted cherries, if in season. Dust with a little icing sugar, if liked, and squeeze over the lime juice. Serve chilled.

roasted summer vegetables

Serves **4**
Preparation time **15 minutes**
Cooking time **45–50 minutes**

1 **red pepper**, cored,
    deseeded and thickly sliced
1 **yellow pepper**, cored,
    deseeded and thickly sliced
1 **aubergine**, cut into chunks
2 **yellow** or **green courgettes**,
    cut into chunks
1 **red onion**, cut into wedges
6 **garlic cloves**
150 g (5 oz) **yellow** and **red**
    baby plum tomatoes
2 tablespoons **extra virgin**
    rapeseed or **olive oil**
4–5 **thyme sprigs**
150 g (5 oz) **hazelnuts**
125 g (4 oz) **rocket leaves**
2 tablespoons **raspberry** or
    balsamic vinegar
salt and **pepper**
handful of **mustard cress**,
    to garnish (optional)

Toss all the vegetables, except the tomatoes, in a large bowl with the oil. Season with a little salt and pepper and add the thyme. Tip into a large roasting tin and place in a preheated oven, 190°C (375°F), Gas Mark 5, for 40–45 minutes or until the vegetables are tender. Add the tomatoes and return to the oven for a further 5 minutes or until the tomatoes are just softened and beginning to burst.

Meanwhile, tip the hazelnuts into a small roasting tin and place in the oven for about 10–12 minutes or until golden and the skin is peeling away. Leave to cool, then remove the excess skin and crush lightly.

Toss the rocket leaves gently with the mixed, roasted vegetables and heap on to large plates. Scatter over the crushed hazelnuts and drizzle with the vinegar. Scatter over the mustard cress, if using, and serve immediately,

For roasted vegetable pasta sauce, roast the vegetables as above, then tip into a large saucepan with the rest of the vegetables, 500 ml (17 fl oz) passata and 150 ml (¼ pint) vegetable stock. Bring to the boil, then reduce the heat and simmer gently for 20 minutes. Remove from the heat and use a hand-held blender to blend until smooth. Season with salt and pepper, to taste, and serve with bowls of hot pasta. Alternatively, stir in an extra 250 ml (8 fl oz) vegetable stock to make soup.

middle eastern bread salad

Serves **4–6**

Preparation time **10 minutes**,
  plus cooling

Cooking time **2–3 minutes**

2 **wholemeal flatbreads** or
  flour tortillas

1 large **green pepper**, cored,
  deseeded and diced

1 **Lebanese cucumber**, diced

250 g (8 oz) **cherry tomatoes**,
  halved

½ **red onion**, finely chopped

2 tablespoons chopped **mint**

2 tablespoons chopped
  parsley

2 tablespoons chopped
  coriander

3 tablespoons **olive oil**

juice of 1 **lemon**

salt and **pepper**

Toast the flatbreads or tortillas on a preheated ridged griddle pan or under a preheated hot grill for 2–3 minutes or until charred. Leave to cool, then tear into bite-sized pieces.

Put the green pepper, cucumber, tomatoes, onion and herbs in a serving bowl, add the oil and lemon juice and season with salt and pepper, tossing well. Add the bread and stir again. Serve immediately.

For tomato & bread salad, chop 750 g (1½ lb) tomatoes and put into a large bowl. Add 4 slices of diced day-old bread, 1 bunch of basil leaves, 125 g (4 oz) pitted black olives, 75 ml (3 fl oz) olive oil, 1 tablespoon balsamic vinegar and salt and pepper. Toss well and serve.

pepper & aubergine hummus

Serves **4–6**
Preparation time **10 minutes**,
  plus cooling
Cooking time **45–50 minutes**

1 **red pepper**, cored,
  deseeded and quartered
3 **garlic cloves**, unpeeled and
  lightly crushed
1 **aubergine**, cut into large
  chunks
1 tablespoon **chilli oil**, plus
  extra to serve
½ tablespoon **fennel seeds**
  (optional)
400 g (13 oz) can **chickpeas**,
  drained
1 tablespoon **tahini**
1 teaspoon **sesame seeds**,
  lightly toasted
salt and **pepper**

To serve
4 **wholemeal pitta breads**
olive oil spray
1 teaspoon **paprika**

Put the pepper, garlic and aubergine in a single layer in a large roasting tin. Drizzle with the chilli oil and sprinkle with the fennel seeds, if using, and season with salt and pepper. Place in a preheated oven, 190°C (375°F), Gas Mark 5, for 35–40 minutes or until softened and golden. Remove from the oven but do not turn it off.

Peel the skins from the garlic cloves and put in a food processor or blender with the roasted vegetables, three-quarters of the chickpeas and the tahini. Blend until almost smooth, season to taste and then spoon into a serving bowl. Cover with clingfilm and leave to cool.

Cut the pitta bread into 2.5 cm (1 inch) strips and place in a large bowl. Spray with a little olive oil and toss with the paprika and a little salt until well coated. Arrange in a single layer on a baking sheet. Toast in the oven for 10–12 minutes or until crisp.

Sprinkle the hummus with the remaining chickpeas and the sesame seeds and drizzle with 1–2 tablespoons chilli oil. Serve with the toasted pitta breads.

For roasted artichoke & pepper hummus, replace the aubergine with a drained 400 g (13 oz) can artichoke hearts in water. Roast in the oven with the peppers and garlic, as above, replacing the chilli oil with 1 tablespoon lemon-infused oil. Omit the fennel seeds. Continue as above.

chicken tikka sticks & fennel raita

Serves **6**

Preparation time **20 minutes**, plus marinating and chilling

Cooking time **8–10 minutes**

1 **onion**, finely chopped

½–1 large **red** or **green chilli**, deseeded and finely chopped (to taste)

1.5 cm (¾ inch) piece of **fresh root ginger**, finely chopped

2 **garlic cloves**, finely chopped

150 g (5 oz) **fat-free natural yogurt**

3 teaspoons **mild curry paste**

4 tablespoons chopped **coriander**

4 **chicken breasts**, about 150 g (5 oz) each, cubed

Fennel raita

1 small **fennel bulb**, about 200 g (7 oz)

200 g (7 oz) **fat-free natural yogurt**

3 tablespoons chopped **coriander**

salt and **pepper**

Mix the onion, chilli, ginger and garlic together in a shallow china or glass dish. Add the yogurt, curry paste and coriander and mix together.

Add the cubed chicken to the yogurt mixture, mix to coat, cover with clingfilm and chill for at least 2 hours.

Make the raita. Cut the core away from the fennel and finely chop the remainder, including any green tops. Mix the fennel with the yogurt and coriander and season with salt and pepper. Spoon the raita into a serving dish, cover with clingfilm and chill until needed.

Thread the chicken on to 12 skewers and place them on a foil-lined grill rack. Cook under a preheated grill for 8–10 minutes, turning once, or until browned and the chicken is cooked through. Transfer to serving plates and serve with the raita on the side.

For a red pepper & almond chutney, to serve with the skewers instead of the raita, blend 75 g (3 oz) shop-bought roasted peppers in a blender or food processor, with a handful of mint leaves, 1 chopped garlic clove and ½ teaspoon chilli powder. Blend until smooth, then add salt to taste and 1½ tablespoons toasted flaked almonds. Pulse a couple of times to roughly crush the almonds and stir in 1 tablespoon chopped coriander.

salmon & cucumber sushi

Serves **4**

Preparation time **15 minutes**, plus cooling

Cooking time **about 15 minutes**

300 g (10 oz) **sushi rice**

2 tablespoons **rice vinegar**

1 tablespoon **caster sugar**

2 **nori sheets**

1 teaspoon **wasabi paste**

2 long strips of **cucumber**, the length of the nori and about 1 cm (½ inch) thick

100 g (3½ oz) **smoked salmon**

2 tablespoons **pickled ginger**

4 tablespoons **soy sauce**

Cook the sushi rice according to the packet instructions.

Mix together the vinegar and sugar in a bowl and stir until the sugar dissolves. Once the rice is cooked, and when it is still warm, mix in enough of the vinegar and sugar mixture to coat the rice grains, but do not allow the rice to become wet. Tip the rice on to a tray to cool quickly.

Take 1 nori sheet and place it on a bamboo mat with the longest side in line with your body and the ridged surface facing upwards. With damp hands, cover three-quarters of the nori sheet with a thin layer of rice, leaving a band of nori at the top without rice.

Spread a little wasabi paste with your finger on top of the rice in a thin line, at the edge nearest to you. Then place a cucumber strip and some smoked salmon on the wasabi.

Use the bamboo mat to start rolling the nori up, tucking in the cucumber and salmon as you go. Once you have rolled up the majority of the nori, wet your finger and dampen the plain edge of nori. Finish rolling up the nori. The wet edge will stick the roll together. Repeat with the other nori sheet. Then, using a sharp knife, cut the rolls into 8 even pieces or 4 even pieces and 1 slightly larger piece cut into 2 on the diagonal.

Mix the remaining wasabi and soy sauce and serve with the pickled ginger alongside the nori rolls.

turkey croque madame

Serves **4**
Preparation time **10 minutes**
Cooking time **8–10 minutes**

8 slices of **wholegrain bread**
from a large, round loaf
3 tablespoons **wholegrain mustard**
200 g (7 oz) **aged Gruyère**
or **reduced-fat mature Cheddar cheese**, finely grated
200 g (7 oz) **cooked turkey**, thinly sliced
2 **tomatoes**, sliced
2 **spring onions**, thinly sliced
4 tablespoons l**ow-fat cream cheese** (optional)
1 tablespoon **distilled vinegar**
4 **large eggs**
100 g (3½ oz) **baby leaf spinach**
pepper
chopped **chives**, to garnish

Lay 4 slices of the bread on a board and spread each slice with the mustard. Top the slices with half of the Gruyère or Cheddar, the turkey and tomato slices, then scatter with the spring onions. Season with pepper and scatter over the remaining Gruyère or Cheddar. Spread the cream cheese, if using, over the remaining slices of bread and place, cheese side down, on top of the sandwiches.

Heat a large, nonstick frying pan over a medium heat until hot, then carefully add the sandwiches and cook for 4–5 minutes or until golden and crispy. Turn the sandwiches over and cook for a further 4–5 minutes. Alternatively, toast in a flat-surfaced panini machine according to the manufacturer's instructions.

Meanwhile, bring a large saucepan of water to a gentle simmer, add the vinegar and stir with a large spoon to create a swirl. Carefully break 2 eggs into the water and cook for 3 minutes. Remove with a slotted spoon and keep warm. Repeat with the remaining eggs.

Transfer each sandwich to a serving plate, scatter over a few spinach leaves and top with a poached egg. Garnish with chives and serve immediately.

For turkey & cheese sandwiches, cut 1 large wholegrain baguette almost in half lengthways. Cut into 4 and place, opened out, on a baking sheet. Top as above with the mustard, turkey, tomatoes and spring onions. Omit the cream cheese and finish with all of the grated cheese. Cook under a preheated hot grill for 3–4 minutes or until hot and melted. Serve hot with baby leaf spinach and poached eggs, if liked.

lamb kefta pittas

Serves **4**
Preparation time **20 minutes**
Cooking time **10–12 minutes**

½ tablespoon **groundnut oil**
4 **wholemeal pitta breads**
lemon juice, to serve

Lamb keftas

1 **small onion**, chopped
2 **garlic cloves**, crushed
400 g (13 oz) **minced lamb**
50 g (2 oz) **fresh wholemeal
breadcrumbs**
1 **small egg**, lightly beaten
1 small bunch of **parsley**,
chopped
1 small bunch of **coriander**,
chopped
¼ tablespoon **ground
cinnamon**
1 tablespoon **ground paprika**
½ tablespoon **ground cumin**
salt and **pepper**

Salad

1 **carrot**, peeled and coarsely
grated
6 **radishes**, thinly sliced
½ **iceberg lettuce**, shredded
½ **cucumber**, thinly sliced

Place all the kefta ingredients in a food processor
and pulse several times until well combined. Tip into
a large bowl and, using wet hands, shape the mixture
into 16 meatballs.

Heat the oil in a large, nonstick frying pan over a
medium heat, add the meatballs and then fry for
10–12 minutes, turning frequently, until cooked
through and browned all over. Remove with a slotted
spoon and drain on kitchen paper.

Meanwhile, wrap the pitta breads in foil and place in
a preheated oven, 180°C (350°F), Gas Mark 4, for
5–8 minutes or until warm. To make the salad, mix the
carrot, radishes, lettuce and cucumber in a bowl.

Split open the warmed pittas, fill with the salad and
then add the meatballs. Squeeze over a little lemon
juice and serve immediately.

For barbecued lamb skewers, make the kefta
mixture as above. Tip into a large bowl and form into
flat sausage shapes around 4 long, flat metal skewers.
Cook on a barbecue for 10–12 minutes or until cooked
through, then serve with the pitta breads and salad
as above.

griddled chicken baguettes

Serves **4**
Preparation time **10 minutes**
Cooking time **8–10 minutes**

4 small **part-baked granary** or
  seeded baguettes
2 large boneless, skinless
  chicken breasts, about
  300 g (10 oz) in total
1 teaspoon **olive oil**
4 tablespoons **red pepper
  pesto**
2 tablespoons **sunflower
  seeds**
handful of **rocket leaves**
salt and **pepper**

Salad
¼ **cucumber**, halved,
  deseeded and thinly sliced
2 tablespoons chopped **mint**
1 tablespoon **lemon juice**

Place the baguettes on a baking sheet and bake in a preheated oven, 200°C (400°F), Gas Mark 6, for 8–10 minutes, or according to the packet instructions, until crisp.

Meanwhile, lay a chicken breast between 2 sheets of clingfilm and flatten with a rolling pin or meat mallet. Repeat with the remaining chicken breast. Heat a griddle pan over a medium-high heat until hot. Rub the oil over the chicken breasts, season with salt and pepper and cook on the hot griddle for 2–3 minutes or until slightly charred. Turn the chicken breasts over and cook for a further 2–3 minutes or until slightly charred and cooked through but not dry. Remove from the pan, cover with foil and leave to rest.

Make the salad. Mix together the cucumber, mint, lemon juice and a little salt and pepper in a small bowl.

Slice the chicken into thick slices. Cut the baguettes in half lengthways, spread with the red pepper pesto, then fill with the chicken and the cucumber salad. Sprinkle with sunflower seeds and add a few rocket leaves. Cut in half and serve immediately.

For griddled chicken & spicy couscous, prepare and cook 4 chicken breasts as above and cut into thick slices. Meanwhile, cook 500 g (1 lb) wholewheat couscous according to the packet instructions, then fork through 2 tablespoons harissa (see page 94 for homemade). Serve the chicken on the couscous with the cucumber salad as above.

felafel pitta pockets

Serves **4**
Preparation time **15 minutes**,
   plus overnight soaking
Cooking time **12 minutes**

250 g (8 oz) **dried chickpeas**
1 **small onion**, finely chopped
2 **garlic cloves**, crushed
½ bunch of **parsley**
½ bunch of **coriander**
2 teaspoons **ground
   coriander**
½ teaspoon **baking powder**
vegetable oil, for shallow-
   frying
4 **wholemeal pitta breads**
handful of **salad leaves**
2 **tomatoes**, diced
4 tablespoons **fat-free Greek
   yogurt**
salt and **pepper**

Put the chickpeas in a bowl, add cold water to cover by a generous 10 cm (4 inches) and leave to soak overnight.

Drain the chickpeas, transfer to a food processor and process until coarsely ground. Add the onion, garlic, fresh herbs, ground coriander and baking powder. Season with salt and pepper and process until really smooth. Using wet hands, shape the mixture into 16 small patties.

Heat a little vegetable oil in a large frying pan over a medium-high heat, add the patties, in batches, and fry for 3 minutes on each side or until golden and cooked through. Remove with a slotted spoon and drain on kitchen paper.

Split the pitta breads and fill with the felafel, salad leaves and diced tomatoes. Add a spoonful of the yogurt to each and serve immediately.

For felafel salad, toss 4 handfuls of mixed salad leaves with a little olive oil, lemon juice and salt and pepper and arrange on serving plates. Core, deseed and dice 1 red pepper and sprinkle it over the salads. Top with the felafel and spoon over a little yogurt.

smoked mackerel crostini

Serves **4**
Preparation time **10 minutes**
Cooking time **2–3 minutes**

230 g (7½ oz) **smoked
    mackerel fillets**, skinned
1 tablespoon **creamed
    horseradish**
2 tablespoons **half-fat crème
    fraîche**
1 tablespoon chopped **chives**
finely grated rind of 1 **lemon**
1 tablespoon **lemon juice**
1 **granary** or **seeded
    baguette**, sliced
1 **spring onion**, finely sliced
    diagonally (optional)
4 **little gem lettuces**, leaves
    separated
pepper

Put the smoked mackerel in a bowl and break into
flakes with a fork. Add the horseradish, crème fraîche,
chives, lemon rind and juice and plenty of pepper and
mix together gently.

Place the sliced baguette on a grill pan and cook under
a preheated medium-hot grill for 2–3 minutes or until
crisp and golden, turning once. Serve the hot crostini
immediately with the smoked mackerel rillettes, spring
onion, if liked, and the lettuce leaves.

For smoked mackerel fishcakes, mix the flaked
mackerel with 230 g (7½ oz) cold mashed potato,
1½ tablespoons horseradish, the chives, lemon rind and
pepper, omitting the crème fraîche and lemon juice. Chill
for 1 hour. Form into 4 patties with slightly damp hands,
then dust in flour. Blitz the baguette in a food processor
or blender to make breadcrumbs. Dip each fishcake
in beaten egg and coat in the breadcrumbs. Heat a
little extra virgin rapeseed oil in a frying pan, add the
fishcakes and fry for 4–5 minutes on each side or until
cooked through and crisp. Drain on kitchen paper and
serve with mixed salad leaves.

tuna & jalapeño baked potatoes

Serves **4**

Preparation time **10 minutes**, plus cooling

Cooking time **1 hour 5 minutes**

4 large **baking potatoes**

2 x 160 g (5½ oz) cans **tuna** in spring water, drained

2 tablespoons drained and chopped **green jalapeño peppers** in brine

2 **spring onions**, finely chopped

4 firm, ripe **tomatoes**, deseeded and chopped

2 tablespoons chopped **chives**

3 tablespoons **low-fat soured cream**

100 g (3½ oz) **reduced-fat extra mature Cheddar cheese**, grated

salt and **pepper**

Prick the potatoes all over with the tip of a sharp knife and place directly in a preheated oven, 180°C (350°F), Gas Mark 4, for 1 hour or until crisp on the outside and the inside is tender. Leave until cool enough to handle.

Cut the potatoes in half and scoop the cooked flesh into a bowl. Place the empty potato skins, cut side up, on a baking sheet. Mix the tuna, jalapeño peppers, spring onions, tomatoes and chives into the potato in the bowl. Gently fold in the soured cream, then season with salt and pepper to taste.

Spoon the filling into the potato skins, sprinkle with the Cheddar and cook under a preheated medium-hot grill for 4–5 minutes or until hot and melted. Serve immediately with a frisée salad.

For spicy tuna wraps, spoon 4 tablespoons chunky spicy tomato salsa on to 4 large, wholemeal flour tortillas. Scatter with the tuna, jalapeño peppers and spring onions. Omit the tomatoes, chives and Cheddar and top with ½ shredded iceberg lettuce. Roll up the wraps tightly and cut in half diagonally. Serve with a little low-fat soured cream, if liked.

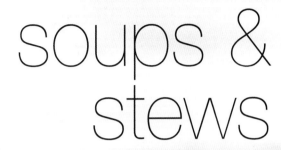

soups & stews

spring minestrone

Serves **4–6**
Preparation time **15 minutes**
Cooking time **55 minutes**

2 tablespoons **olive oil**
1 **onion**, thinly sliced
2 **carrots**, peeled and diced
2 **celery sticks**, diced
2 **garlic cloves**, peeled
1 **potato**, peeled and diced
125 g (4 oz) **peas** or **broad
  beans**, thawed if frozen
1 **courgette**, diced
125 g (4 oz) **green beans**,
  trimmed and cut into 3.5 cm
  (1½ inch) pieces
125 g (4 oz) **plum tomatoes**,
  skinned and chopped
1.2 litres (2 pints) **vegetable
  stock**
75 g (3 oz) **small pasta
  shapes**
10 **basil leaves**, torn
salt and **pepper**

To serve
olive oil
grated **Parmesan cheese**

Heat the oil in a large, heavy-based saucepan over a low heat, add the onion, carrots, celery and garlic and cook, stirring occasionally, for 10 minutes. Add the potato, peas or broad beans, courgette and green beans and cook, stirring frequently, for 2 minutes. Add the tomatoes, season with salt and pepper and cook for a further 2 minutes.

Pour in the stock and bring to the boil, then reduce the heat and simmer gently for 20 minutes or until all the vegetables are very tender.

Add the pasta and basil to the soup and cook, stirring frequently, until the pasta is al dente. Season with salt and pepper to taste.

Ladle into bowls, drizzle with olive oil and sprinkle with the Parmesan. Serve with toasted country bread or Parmesan toasts (see below).

For Parmesan toasts, to serve as an accompaniment, toast 4–6 slices of ciabatta on one side only under a preheated medium grill. Brush the other side with 2–3 tablespoons olive oil and sprinkle with chilli flakes and 2 tablespoons grated Parmesan cheese, then cook under the preheated grill until golden and crisp.

chicken & tofu miso noodles

Serves **4**
Preparation time **10 minutes**
Cooking time **25 minutes**

2 x 10 g sachets **instant miso soup powder** or **paste**
750 ml (1¼ pints) **water**
2 **star anise**
2 tablespoons **fish sauce**
1 tablespoon **light soy sauce**
1 tablespoon **palm sugar** or **soft light brown sugar**
1 **red chilli**, deseeded and sliced (optional)
200 g (7 oz) **baby corn**
125 g (4 oz) **mangetout**
250 g (8 oz) **cooked chicken breast**, torn
200 g (7 oz) **firm silken tofu**, cut into 1 cm (½ inch) cubes
160 g (5½ oz) **enoki mushrooms**, or **shiitake mushrooms**, thinly sliced
400 g (13 oz) **fresh egg noodles**
1 **spring onion**, very finely sliced, to garnish (optional)

Place the miso powder or paste in a large saucepan with the measurement water, star anise, fish sauce, soy sauce, sugar and chilli, if using. Bring to the boil, then reduce the heat and simmer gently for 15 minutes.

Stir in the baby corn and mangetout and cook for a further 3 minutes or until almost tender. Remove the pan from the heat, stir in the chicken, tofu and mushrooms and cover to retain the heat.

Cook the noodles in a large saucepan of boiling water for 3–4 minutes, or according to the packet instructions, until tender. Drain well and divide between deep bowls, then ladle over the hot soup and serve immediately, garnished with the spring onion, if liked.

For chicken, tofu & mushroom stir-fry, heat 2 tablespoons groundnut oil in a smoking hot wok or large frying pan. Stir-fry the baby corn and mangetout for 2 minutes or until beginning to wilt. Add the chicken, tofu and mushrooms and stir-fry for 1–2 minutes or until hot and the mushrooms are tender. Stir in a 350 g (11½ oz) jar of black bean stir-fry sauce, toss briefly and serve with the cooked noodles, sprinkled with spring onions.

squash, kale & mixed bean soup

Serves **6**
Preparation time **15 minutes**
Cooking time **45 minutes**

1 tablespoon **olive oil**
1 **onion**, finely chopped
2 **garlic cloves**, finely
  chopped
1 teaspoon **smoked paprika**
500 g (1 lb) **butternut
  squash**, halved, deseeded,
  peeled and diced
2 small **carrots**, peeled and
  diced
500 g (1 lb) **tomatoes**,
  skinned (optional) and
  roughly chopped
400 g (13 oz) can **mixed
  beans**, drained
900 ml (1 ½ pints) **vegetable**
  or **chicken stock**
150 ml (¼ pint) **half-fat
  crème fraîche**
100 g (3½ oz) **kale**, torn into
  bite-sized pieces
salt and **pepper**

Heat the oil in a saucepan over a medium-low heat, add the onion and fry gently for 5 minutes. Stir in the garlic and smoked paprika and cook briefly, then add the squash, carrots, tomatoes and mixed beans.

Pour in the stock, season with salt and pepper and bring to the boil, stirring frequently. Reduce the heat, cover and simmer for 25 minutes or until the vegetables are tender.

Stir in the crème fraîche, then add the kale, pressing it just beneath the surface of the stock. Cover and cook for 5 minutes or until the kale has just wilted. Ladle into bowls and serve with warm garlic bread.

For cheesy squash, pepper & mixed bean soup,
make as above, replacing the carrots with 1 cored, deseeded and diced red pepper. Pour in the stock, then add 65 g (2½ oz) Parmesan cheese rinds and season. Cover and simmer for 25 minutes. Stir in the crème fraîche but omit the kale. Discard the Parmesan rinds, ladle the soup into bowls and top with grated Parmesan.

pesto & lemon soup

Serves **6**
Preparation time **10 minutes**
Cooking time **25 minutes**

1 tablespoon **olive oil**
1 **onion**, finely chopped
2 **garlic cloves**, finely chopped
2 **tomatoes**, skinned and
   chopped
1.2 litres (2 pints) **vegetable
   stock**
3 teaspoons **pesto**, plus extra
   to serve
grated rind and juice of
   1 **lemon**
100 g (3½ oz) **broccoli**, cut
   into small florets, stems
   sliced
150 g (5 oz) **courgettes**,
   diced
100 g (3½ oz) **frozen green
   soya beans**
65 g (2½ oz) **small pasta
   shapes**
50 g (2 oz) **spinach**, shredded
salt and **pepper**
handful of **basil leaves**, to
   garnish (optional)

Heat the oil in a saucepan over a medium-low heat, add the onion and fry gently for 5 minutes, stirring occasionally, until softened. Add the garlic, tomatoes, stock, pesto, lemon rind and a little salt and pepper and bring to the boil, then reduce the heat and simmer gently for 10 minutes.

Add the broccoli, courgettes, soya beans and pasta shapes and simmer for 6 minutes. Add the spinach and lemon juice and cook for a further 2 minutes or until the spinach has just wilted and the pasta is al dente.

Ladle into bowls, top with extra spoonfuls of pesto and sprinkle with basil leaves. Serve with warm olive or sun-dried tomato focaccia or ciabatta bread or Parmesan thins (see below).

For homemade Parmesan thins, to serve as an accompaniment, line a baking sheet with nonstick baking paper, then sprinkle 100 g (3½ oz) grated Parmesan cheese into 18 well-spaced mounds. Cook in a preheated oven, 190°C (375°F), Gas Mark 5, for about 5 minutes or until the cheese has melted and is just beginning to brown. Leave to cool and harden, then peel off the paper and serve on the side with the soup.

thai-style chicken soup

Serves **4**
Preparation time **10 minutes**
Cooking time **25 minutes**

1 litre (1¾ pints) **chicken
  stock**
4 tablespoons **Thai fish sauce**
1 tablespoon **palm sugar** or
  soft light brown sugar
2 **lemon grass stalks**, sliced
  in half lengthways
50 g (2 oz) **galangal** or **fresh
  root ginger**, peeled and
  finely sliced
1 large bunch of **coriander**,
  finely chopped, leaves and
  stalks separate
250 g (8 oz) boneless,
  skinless **chicken thighs**,
  cut into strips
225 g (7½ oz) can **bamboo
  shoots**, drained (optional)
200 g (7 oz) **vermicelli rice
  noodles**

Put the stock, fish sauce, sugar, lemon grass and
galangal or ginger in a large saucepan and bring
to the boil, then reduce the heat and simmer gently
for 15 minutes. Strain through a sieve to remove the
galangal or ginger and lemon grass. Return the liquid
to the pan and stir in the chopped coriander stalks.

Add the chicken and simmer gently for a further
4–5 minutes or until cooked through. Add the bamboo
shoots, if using.

Meanwhile, put the noodles in a large saucepan of
boiling water, turn off the heat and leave to stand for
4 minutes, or according to the packet instructions,
until tender. Drain well and divide between deep bowls.
Ladle over the chicken soup, sprinkle with the chopped
coriander leaves and serve immediately.

For chicken & bamboo shoot curry, heat
1 tablespoon groundnut oil in a wok or large frying
pan, add 2 tablespoons green curry paste and fry for
2 minutes, stirring constantly. Add 300 ml (½ pint)
reduced-fat coconut milk and 150 ml (¼ pint) chicken
stock, the fish sauce, palm sugar, chopped coriander
stalks and chicken, omitting the lemon grass and
galangal or fresh root ginger. Simmer gently for about
10 minutes, or until the chicken is cooked through,
adding the bamboo shoots 4 minutes before the end
of the cooking time. Serve with the chopped coriander
leaves and steamed Thai rice.

butter bean & tomato soup

Serves **4**
Preparation time **10 minutes**
Cooking time **20 minutes**

3 tablespoons **olive oil**
1 **onion**, finely chopped
2 **celery sticks**, thinly sliced
2 **garlic cloves**, thinly sliced
2 x 400 g (13 oz) cans **butter beans**, drained
4 tablespoons **sun-dried tomato paste**
900 ml (1½ pints) **vegetable stock**
1 tablespoon chopped **thyme** or **rosemary**, plus extra leaves to garnish
salt and **pepper**
Parmesan cheese shavings, to serve

Heat the oil in a saucepan over a medium heat, add the onion and fry for 3 minutes or until softened. Add the celery and garlic and fry for 2 minutes.

Add the butter beans, sun-dried tomato paste, stock, rosemary or thyme and season with salt and pepper. Bring to the boil, then reduce the heat, cover and simmer gently for 15 minutes.

Ladle into bowls and serve sprinkled with the Parmesan and extra thyme or rosemary leaves. This soup makes a light main course served with bread and plenty of Parmesan.

For spiced carrot & lentil soup, heat 2 tablespoons oil in a saucepan, add 1 chopped onion, 2 crushed garlic cloves and 375 g (12 oz) chopped carrots and fry for 10 minutes. Add a 400 g (13 oz) can lentils, drained, 2 teaspoons ground coriander, 1 teaspoon ground cumin and 1 tablespoon chopped thyme and fry for 1 minute. Stir in 1 litre (1¾ pints) vegetable stock, a 400 g (13 oz) can chopped tomatoes and 2 teaspoons lemon juice and bring to the boil. Cover and simmer gently for 20 minutes. Put in a food processor or blender and blend until smooth, then return to the pan and warm through.

prawn & pork wonton soup

Serves **4**
Preparation time **25 minutes**
Cooking time **5–6 minutes**

100 g (3½ oz) **minced pork**
150 g (5 oz) **raw peeled prawns**
4 **spring onions**, finely chopped
1 **garlic clove**
1 cm (½ inch) piece of **fresh root ginger**, peeled and chopped
1 tablespoon **oyster sauce**
20 **wonton wrappers**
750 ml (1¼ pints) **chicken stock**
1 head of **Chinese spring greens**, shredded
1–2 tablespoons **fish sauce**

To serve
handful of **coriander leaves**
1 tablespoon **sesame seeds**
lime wedges

Place the pork, prawns, 2 of the spring onions, the garlic, ginger and oyster sauce in a food processor or blender and blend to a paste.

Take 1 of the wonton wrappers and place 1 teaspoon of the prawn and pork mixture in the centre. Dampen the edges of the wrapper with a little water and bring them up around the filling, enclosing it completely in a little bundle. Repeat with the remainder of the wrappers and prawn and pork mixture.

Bring the stock to the boil in a large saucepan, then reduce the heat, add the wontons and simmer for 4–5 minutes. Remove 1 of the wontons and check that it has become firm to the touch, which will indicate that it is cooked.

Add the spring greens to the pan and cook for 1 minute, then season with the fish sauce.

Ladle into deep bowls and serve with a few coriander leaves, a sprinkling of sesame seeds and a lime wedge on the side.

For sesame wontons with soy dipping sauce, make the wontons as above and steam them in a bamboo steamer for 5 minutes. Remove the wontons from the steamer and sprinkle over 2 tablespoons sesame seeds. Make a dipping sauce by mixing together 3 tablespoons light soy sauce, 2 teaspoons peeled and grated fresh root ginger, 1 finely sliced red chilli and 1 tablespoon fish sauce.

hot & sour beef broth

Serves **4**
Preparation time **12 minutes**
Cooking time **about**
15 minutes

1 litre (1¾ pints) **clear beef stock**
3 tablespoons **fish sauce**
1 tablespoon **rice vinegar**
1 tablespoon **lime juice**
1 tablespoon **palm sugar** or **soft light brown sugar**
1 **garlic clove**, sliced
2.5 cm (1 inch) piece of **fresh root ginger**, peeled and cut into very thin matchsticks
1 small **red chilli**, deseeded and finely sliced
1 **shallot**, thinly sliced
3 **kaffir lime leaves**, thinly shredded
2 teaspoons **tamarind paste**
100 g (3½ oz) **baby corn**, halved lengthways
350 g (11½ oz) **beef fillet**, thinly sliced
1 **spring onion**, finely sliced, to garnish

Put the stock, fish sauce, vinegar, lime juice and palm sugar in a large saucepan and bring to the boil. Add the garlic, ginger, chilli, shallot, lime leaves, tamarind paste and baby corn, then reduce the heat and simmer gently for 10 minutes.

Stir in the beef fillet, then immediately ladle into bowls. Scatter over the spring onion and serve immediately.

For hot & sour mushroom broth, replace the beef stock and beef fillet with 75 g (3 oz) dried shiitake mushrooms soaked in 1 litre (1¾ pints) boiling vegetable stock for 15–20 minutes. Drain, reserving the soaking liquid, and slice the mushrooms, then make the broth as above.

vegetable broth & sea bass

Serves **4**
Preparation time **5 minutes**
Cooking time **7–8 minutes**

750 ml (1 ¼ pints) **chicken** or **vegetable stock**
1 **fennel bulb**, cut into 8 wedges, herby tops reserved (optional)
12 fine **asparagus spears**
150 g (5 oz) **frozen peas**, thawed
150 g (5 oz) **broad beans**, podded
2 tablespoons **olive oil**
4 **sea bass fillets**, about 200 g (7 oz) each, skin on and pin-boned
small handful of **mint leaves**, torn
small handful of **basil leaves**, torn
salt and **pepper**

Put the stock in a large saucepan and bring to the boil. Add the fennel, reduce the heat and simmer for 3 minutes or until almost tender. Add the asparagus, peas and broad beans and cook for a 1–2 minutes. Season with salt and pepper.

Meanwhile, heat the oil in a frying pan over a medium heat. Season the sea bass with salt and pepper and place, skin side down, in the pan. Cook for 3–4 minutes or until the skin is crispy, then turn the fish over and cook for a further minute.

Ladle the vegetable broth into bowls and sprinkle with a few torn mint and basil leaves. Top the broth with the pan-fried sea bass and reserved herby fennel tops, if liked, and serve.

For Thai broth with prawns, peel and devein 500 g (1 lb) raw tiger prawns, reserving the shells and heads. Heat 750 ml (1 ¼ pints) fish or chicken stock in a saucepan. Add the prawn shells and heads, 2 roughly chopped lemon grass stalks, a 5 cm (2 inch) piece of fresh root ginger, 1 dried red chilli and 2 kaffir lime leaves. Remove the pan from the heat and leave the stock to infuse for 30 minutes. Strain the stock and return it to a clean saucepan. Add the prawns and poach for 3–4 minutes or until they have turned pink and are cooked through. Add 125 g (4 oz) sugar snap peas 1 minute before the end of the cooking time.

vegetable broth with pearl barley

Serves **4**

Preparation time **15 minutes**

Cooking time **1½ hours**

100 g (3½ oz) **pearl barley**

2 tablespoons **extra virgin rapeseed oil**

1 large **onion**, finely chopped

2 **leeks**, trimmed, cleaned and finely chopped

1 **celery stick**, finely chopped

750 g (1½ lb) mixed root vegetables such as **parsnips**, **swede**, **turnips**, **carrots** and **potatoes**, evenly diced

1.2 litres (2 pints) **beef** or **vegetable stock**

1 **bouquet garni**

salt and **pepper**

Bring a large saucepan of water to the boil and pour in the pearl barley. Cook at a gentle simmer for 1 hour. Drain well.

Meanwhile, heat the oil in a large, heavy-based saucepan over a medium-low heat, add the onion, leeks and celery and fry gently for 8–10 minutes or until softened but not coloured. Add the root vegetables and cook for a further 5 minutes, stirring regularly.

Pour in the stock, add the bouquet garni and bring to the boil. Stir in the pearl barley, then reduce the heat and simmer for 25–30 minutes or until the vegetables and pearl barley are tender. Remove the bouquet garni and season to taste with salt and pepper. Ladle into bowls and serve with herby bread, if liked.

For creamy vegetable soup, make the broth as above, then use a hand-held blender to blend the soup until smooth, adding extra stock if necessary. Stir in 3 tablespoons half-fat crème fraîche, scatter with thyme leaves and serve with toasted herby bread croutons.

rustic tuscan bean stew

Serves **4**
Preparation time **12 minutes**
Cooking time **45–50 minutes**

1 tablespoon **olive oil**
1 **red onion**, finely chopped
2 **celery sticks**, thinly sliced
1 large **carrot**, peeled and
    finely chopped
1 **red pepper**, cored,
    deseeded and diced
2 **garlic cloves**, chopped
1 tablespoon **tomato purée**
125 ml (4 fl oz) **red wine**
750 ml (1¼ pints) **vegetable
    stock**
400 g (13 oz) can **mixed
    beans** or **Tuscan bean mix**,
    drained
2–3 **thyme sprigs**, chopped
1 **rosemary sprig**, chopped
2 **bay leaves**
100 g (3½ oz) mini
    wholewheat pasta shapes
    or **orzo**
salt and **pepper**

To serve (optional)
olive oil
grated **Parmesan cheese**

Heat the oil in a large, heavy-based saucepan over a medium-low heat, then add the onion, celery, carrot, red pepper and garlic and cook gently for 12–15 minutes or until softened. Add the tomato purée and wine and cook for a further 2–3 minutes.

Stir in the stock, beans, thyme, rosemary and bay leaves and season with salt and pepper. Bring to the boil, then reduce the heat and simmer gently for 20 minutes.

Stir in the pasta shapes and continue to simmer for about 12 minutes or until the pasta is al dente.

Ladle into bowls and serve with a drizzle of olive oil and sprinkled with the Parmesan, if liked.

For hearty Tuscan bean salad, cook the vegetables in the olive oil for 18–20 minutes or until very tender. Toss with the beans and chopped herbs in a large serving bowl and leave to cool. Stir in 3 deseeded and chopped tomatoes and 1–2 tablespoons red wine vinegar, then season with salt and pepper to taste. Toss lightly with a mixed leaf salad and garnish with Parmesan cheese shavings.

spanish fish stew

Serves **4**
Preparation time **12 minutes**
Cooking time **about
25 minutes**

2 tablespoons **olive oil**
1 large **red onion**, sliced
4 **garlic cloves**, chopped
1 teaspoon **smoked paprika**
or **hot smoked paprika**
pinch of **saffron threads**
350 g (11½ oz) **monkfish
fillet**, cut into chunks
250 g (8 oz) **red mullet fillets**,
cut into large chunks
3 tablespoons **dry or medium-
dry Madeira**
250 ml (8 fl oz) **fish** or
vegetable stock
2 tablespoons **tomato purée**
400 g (13 oz) can **chopped
tomatoes**
2 **bay leaves**
750 g (1½ lb) **live mussels**,
scrubbed and debearded
(discard any that don't
shut when tapped) or
250 g (8 oz) **cooked
shelled mussels**
salt and **pepper**
3 tablespoons chopped
parsley, to garnish

Heat the oil in a large, heavy-based saucepan over a medium-low heat, add the onion and garlic and cook gently for 8–10 minutes or until softened.

Stir in the paprika and saffron and cook for a further minute. Stir in the fish, then pour over the Madeira. Add the stock, tomato purée, tomatoes and bay leaves and season with salt and pepper. Bring to the boil, then reduce the heat and simmer gently for 5 minutes.

Stir in the live mussels, cover and cook over a low heat for about 3 minutes or until they have opened. Discard any that remain closed. Alternatively, if using cooked shelled mussels, simmer the stew for 2–3 minutes more, or until the fish is cooked and tender, then stir in the cooked mussels. Cook for 30 seconds or until the mussels are heated through and piping hot.

Ladle into bowls and sprinkle with the parsley. Serve immediately with crusty bread.

For pan-fried red mullet with tomato sauce,
cook the onion and garlic with the spices as above. Pour in the Madeira and add the tomatoes, finely grated rind of ½ lemon, a pinch of sugar and season with salt and pepper. Simmer for 15–20 minutes. Heat 1–2 tablespoons olive oil in a nonstick frying pan, add 500 g (1 lb) red mullet fillets, skin side down, and fry for 2–3 minutes or until crisp. Cover, reduce the heat and cook for a further 2 minutes or until the fish is just cooked through. Serve with the tomato sauce.

tomato & chorizo stew with clams

Serves **4**
Preparation time **15 minutes**
Cooking time **about**
   25 minutes

300 g (10 oz) **chorizo**
   sausage, cut into chunks
1 teaspoon **coriander seeds**,
   crushed
1 tablespoon **fennel seeds**,
   crushed
1 **onion**, finely chopped
1 **red chilli**, deseeded and
   finely chopped
2 **garlic cloves**, finely chopped
50 ml (2 fl oz) **white wine**
400 g (13 oz) can **chopped**
   tomatoes
200 ml (7 fl oz) **fish stock**
500 g (1 lb) **live clams**,
   cleaned (discard any that
   don't shut when tapped)
small handful of **basil leaves**,
   to garnish

Heat a large saucepan over a high heat, add the chorizo and fry until the natural oil has been released and the chorizo is beginning to colour. Remove with a slotted spoon, leaving behind the oil, and set aside.

Add the coriander and fennel seeds to the chorizo oil and fry for 1 minute, then add the onion and chilli and fry until the onion has softened but not coloured. Add the garlic and fry for a further minute.

Pour in the white wine and leave to bubble until just 1 tablespoon of liquid is left. Add the tomatoes and stock and bring to the boil, then return the chorizo to the pan. Tip in the clams, then cover and cook until the clams have opened. Discard any that remain closed.

Ladle into bowls, sprinkle with a few basil leaves and serve with crusty bread, if liked.

For spicy bean stew with pan-fried John Dory, make the stew as above, omitting the clams and chorizo and adding 400 g (13 oz) can haricot beans and 400 g (13 oz) can kidney beans, drained. Pan-fry 2 John Dory fillets and serve with the bean stew.

french summer vegetable stew

Serves **4**
Preparation time **12 minutes**
Cooking time **about**
25 minutes

2 tablespoons **olive oil**
1 **fennel bulb**
3 **shallots**, sliced
3 **garlic cloves**, sliced
2 tablespoons **Pernod**
125 ml (4 fl oz) **dry white**
wine
1 tablespoon chopped **chives**
1 tablespoon chopped **chervil**
1 teaspoon chopped **tarragon**
2 **courgettes**, halved
lengthways and sliced
100 g (3½ oz) **fine green**
beans, trimmed
500 ml (17 fl oz) **vegetable**
stock
16 large, **pitted green olives**
200 g (7 oz) small **cherry**
tomatoes, mixed colours
if possible
1 small bunch of **basil**, leaves
torn
2 lean **back bacon rashers**,
very thinly sliced (optional)
salt and pepper

Heat the oil in a large, heavy-based saucepan over a medium heat. Cut the fennel into quarters lengthways, remove the tough middle and slice each quarter into 3 wedges. Add to the pan and fry for 4–5 minutes or until beginning to soften and colour. Add the shallots and garlic and fry gently for a further 4–5 minutes or until softened and lightly golden.

Stir in the Pernod, white wine and chopped herbs and bubble for 1–2 minutes or until almost evaporated. Add the courgettes and green beans and stir well.

Add enough stock to almost cover the vegetables and scatter with the olives. Bring to the boil, then reduce the heat, cover and simmer gently for 8–10 minutes or until the vegetables are almost tender. Stir in the tomatoes and basil leaves and simmer for a further 3 minutes. Season to taste with salt and pepper.

Place a small, nonstick frying pan over a high heat and add the bacon, if using. Fry for 3 minutes or until crisp. Remove with a slotted spoon and drain on kitchen paper.

Ladle the stew into bowls and scatter with the crispy bacon, if using. Serve with warm, crusty bread, if liked.

For fennel & olive salad, slice 2 fennel bulbs thinly and arrange on a serving plate. Mix together 2 tablespoons red wine vinegar and 3 tablespoons olive oil in a bowl and season with salt and pepper. Drizzle over the fennel and top with the olives. Scatter over 2 tablespoons chopped parsley and the crispy bacon, if liked.

farmhouse sausage & kale stew

Serves **4**
Preparation time **10 minutes**
Cooking time **40 minutes**

1 tablespoon **olive oil**
150 g (5 oz) lean **smoked bacon**, chopped
3–4 lean **herby pork sausages**, about 250 g (8 oz) in total, thickly sliced
1 **onion**, chopped
3 **garlic cloves**, chopped
1 **leek**, trimmed, cleaned and sliced
400 g (13 oz) can **chopped tomatoes**
2 tablespoons **tomato purée**
1 teaspoon **dried oregano**
pinch of **sugar**
300 ml (½ pint) **golden ale** or **chicken stock**
1 large **potato**, about 300 g (10 oz), peeled and roughly diced
400 g (13 oz) can **borlotti beans**, drained
200 g (7 oz) **kale**, shredded
salt and **pepper**
2 tablespoons chopped **parsley**, to garnish

Heat the oil in a large, heavy-based saucepan over a medium-high heat, add the bacon and sausages and cook for 3–4 minutes or until browned. Add the onion, garlic and leek, reduce the heat slightly and cook for 5–6 minutes until softened, stirring occasionally.

Stir in the tomatoes, tomato purée, dried oregano, sugar and ale or stock and bring to the boil. Stir in the potatoes and beans and season with salt and pepper. Reduce the heat, cover and simmer gently for 20 minutes or until the potatoes are almost tender. Stir in the kale, check the seasoning and cook for a further 8–10 minutes or until the kale and potatoes are tender.

Ladle into bowls and sprinkle with the parsley. Serve immediately.

For chicken & chorizo stew, make as above, replacing the bacon with 150 g (5 oz) diced chorizo, the sausages with 250 g (8oz) sliced boneless, skinless chicken thighs, the oregano with 1 teaspoon smoked paprika and the ale or stock with 300 ml (½ pint) red wine. Serve sprinkled with the parsley and a generous squeeze of lemon juice.

tunisian chickpea & lentil stew

Serves **4**
Preparation time **15 minutes**,
   plus overnight soaking
Cooking time **about 2¼ hours**

200 g (7 oz) **dried chickpeas**
2 tablespoons **olive oil**
3 **garlic cloves**, thinly sliced
1 **onion**, thinly sliced
1 **celery stick**, finely diced
2 **small carrots**, peeled and
   finely diced
pinch of **saffron threads**
½ teaspoon **ground turmeric**
½ teaspoon **paprika**
1 teaspoon **ground cumin**
½ teaspoon **ground ginger**
¼ teaspoon **ground
   cinnamon**
125 g (4 oz) **green lentils**,
   rinsed
2 tablespoons **tomato purée**
750 ml (1¼ pints) **lamb** or
   vegetable stock
salt and **pepper**
3–4 tablespoons chopped
   parsley, to garnish
harissa (see right for
   homemade), to serve

Put the chickpeas in a bowl, add cold water to cover by 10 cm (4 inches) and leave to soak overnight.

Drain the chickpeas, rinse under running cold water and drain again. Place the chickpeas in a saucepan of cold water and bring to the boil. Boil rapidly for 10 minutes, then reduce the heat and simmer gently, partially covered, for about 1 hour or until tender, adding more water as necessary. Drain well.

Meanwhile, heat the oil in a large, heavy-based saucepan over a medium-low heat, add the garlic, onion, celery and carrots and cook for 15 minutes, or until softened, stirring frequently. Add the spices and cook for 1–2 minutes, then increase the heat and add the chickpeas, lentils and tomato purée. Pour in the stock and bring to the boil, then reduce the heat and simmer gently for 40–45 minutes.

Spoon the cooked pulses and vegetables into serving bowls and carefully pour the liquid around the side. Sprinkle with parsley and serve with harissa, to taste.

For homemade harissa, soak 25 g (1 oz) dried red chillies in boiling water for 4 hours. Put 1½ tablespoons cumin seeds, 2 teaspoons caraway seeds and 1 tablespoon coriander seeds in a small frying pan and dry-fry until fragrant. Grind to a powder in a mini chopper. Add the soaked chillies, 3 garlic cloves, 100 g (3½ oz) roasted peppers, 2 tablespoons tomato purée, 1 tablespoon aged sherry vinegar, 1 teaspoon hot smoked paprika, 1 teaspoon salt and just enough olive oil to make a paste. Blend until smooth, then store in an airtight jar in the refrigerator for up to 2–3 weeks.

harira

Serves **8–10**
Preparation time **about
25 minutes**, plus overnight
soaking
Cooking time **about 2¾ hours**

250 g (8 oz) **dried chickpeas**
2 **chicken breasts**, halved
1.2 litres (2 pints) **chicken
stock**
1.2 litres (2 pints) **water**
2 x 400 g (13 oz) cans
chopped tomatoes
¼ teaspoon crumbled **saffron
threads** (optional)
2 **onions**, chopped
125 g (4 oz) **long-grain rice**
50 g (2 oz) **green lentils**,
rinsed
2 tablespoons finely chopped
coriander
2 tablespoons finely chopped
parsley
salt and **pepper**
coriander sprigs, to garnish
fat-free natural yogurt,
to serve

Put the chickpeas in a bowl, add cold water to cover
by a generous 10 cm (4 inches) and leave to soak
overnight. Drain the chickpeas, rinse under running
cold water and drain again. Place the chickpeas in
a saucepan of cold water and bring to the boil. Boil
rapidly for 10 minutes, then reduce the heat and
simmer, partially covered, for about 1¾ hours or until
tender, adding more water as necessary. Drain well.

Meanwhile, place the chicken breasts, stock and
measurement water in another saucepan and bring
to the boil, then reduce the heat, cover and simmer
for 10–15 minutes or until the chicken is just cooked.
Remove the chicken with a slotted spoon, reserving the
stock, place it on a board and shred it, discarding the
skin. Set aside.

Stir the chickpeas, tomatoes, saffron, if using, onions,
rice and lentils into the reserved stock in the pan, cover
and simmer for 30–35 minutes or until the rice and
lentils are tender.

Add the shredded chicken, coriander and parsley just
before serving. Heat the soup for a further 5 minutes
without letting it boil. Season to taste with salt and
pepper, then ladle into bowls, drizzle over the yogurt
and garnish with the coriander.

For budget harira, make as above, omitting the
chicken breasts and replacing the saffron with
½ teaspoon ground turmeric and ½ teaspoon
ground cinnamon.

fish & seafood

cod & aubergine tapenade

Serves **4**
Preparation time **12 minutes**
Cooking time **35–40 minutes**

1 **aubergine**, cut into chunks
1 **garlic clove**, sliced
olive oil spray
4 thick, line-caught **cod fillets**,
    about 150 g (5 oz) each
finely grated rind of ½ **lemon**
2 teaspoons finely chopped
    lemon thyme
2 teaspoons **olive oil**
1–2 tablespoons **black olive
    tapenade**
1–2 tablespoons **fat-free
    Greek yogurt**
2 tablespoons **pine nuts,**
    lightly toasted (optional)
salt and **pepper**

Put the aubergine in a foil-lined roasting tin, scatter with the garlic, season with salt and pepper and spray with a little olive oil. Cover tightly with foil and place in a preheated oven, 180°C (350°F), Gas Mark 4, for 35–40 minutes or until the aubergine is tender.

Meanwhile, place a cod fillet in the centre of a piece of foil or nonstick baking paper. Scatter with a little lemon rind, lemon thyme and season with salt and pepper. Drizzle over ½ teaspoon of the olive oil, then fold the foil or paper over several times to make a small parcel. Repeat with the remaining cod fillets. Place the parcels on a baking sheet and bake in the oven 12 minutes before the end of the aubergine cooking time, until the fish is just cooked through. Leave to rest.

Remove the aubergine from the oven and place in a food processor or blender with the black olive tapenade and Greek yogurt. Blend until almost smooth, season to taste and scrape into a bowl.

Serve the cod on a bed of steamed green beans, scattered with the pine nuts, if using, and with the aubergine and yogurt purée on the side.

For baked lemon sole & capers, place 4 lemon sole fillets on a large, foil-lined baking sheet. Sprinkle with the lemon rind, lemon thyme and 1 teaspoon rinsed and drained capers, chopped. Drizzle with the olive oil, then season with pepper. Cover tightly with foil and place in the preheated oven for 8–10 minutes or until the fish is just cooked and flakes easily. Serve as above.

roasted haddock loins

Serves **4**
Preparation time **10 minutes**
Cooking time **about 1 hour**

4 thick **haddock loins**, about
   125 g (4 oz) each
2 tablespoons **olive oil**
2 teaspoons finely grated
   lemon rind
1 teaspoon **fennel seeds**
6 small **tomatoes**, halved
2 **garlic cloves**, chopped
1 teaspoon **dried oregano**
2 tablespoons **balsamic
   vinegar**
750 g (1½ lb) **new potatoes**
olive oil spray
salt and **pepper**
oregano leaves, to garnish

Rub the haddock loins with 1 tablespoon of the oil, the lemon rind and fennel seeds. Place in a roasting tin, sprinkle with a little salt and pepper and leave to marinate in the refrigerator.

Put the tomatoes, cut side up, in one close-fitting layer in a roasting tin. Sprinkle with the garlic, dried oregano and salt and pepper. Drizzle with the balsamic vinegar and remaining oil and place in a preheated oven, 180°C (350°F), Gas Mark 4, for 45 minutes.

Meanwhile, cook the potatoes in a large saucepan of salted boiling water for 18–20 minutes or until tender. Drain, crush lightly with the back of a fork and tip into an ovenproof dish. Spray with a little olive oil and season.

Remove the tomatoes from the oven and keep warm. Increase the oven temperature to 220°C (425°F), Gas Mark 7. Place the potatoes and the haddock loins in the oven for 10–15 minutes or until the fish flakes easily when pressed in the centre with a knife and the potatoes are slightly crispy. Serve the fish with the potatoes and tomatoes, garnished with oregano leaves.

For warm smoked haddock salad, replace the haddock loins with 4 smoked haddock fillets. Roast the fish as above, then break into large flakes. Cook the potatoes in a saucepan of boiling water as above, then cut into thick slices. Mix together 1 tablespoon wholegrain mustard, 1 teaspoon tarragon vinegar and 2 tablespoons half-fat crème fraîche in a bowl. Season, then stir in the potatoes. Pile washed watercress on to serving plates and spoon over the dressed potatoes. Scatter with the flaked haddock and serve.

sea bream & red mullet tagine

Serves **4**
Preparation time **15 minutes**
Cooking time **35–40 minutes**

250 g (8 oz) **sea bream
   fillets**, cut into large chunks
250 g (8 oz) **red mullet fillets**,
   cut into large chunks
5½ tablespoons **chermoula**
   (see below for homemade)
1 tablespoon **olive oil**
1 **onion**, chopped
1 **celery stick**, chopped
1 **yellow pepper**, cored,
   deseeded and sliced
1½ **preserved lemons**,
   chopped
250 g (8 oz) **cherry tomatoes**
400 g (13 oz) can **chickpeas**,
   drained
pinch of **saffron threads**
250 ml (8 fl oz) **fish** or
   vegetable stock
16 large, **pitted green olives**
salt and **pepper**
small handful of **coriander
   leaves**, to garnish

Mix together the fish fillets and 2½ tablespoons of the chermoula in a non-metallic bowl, cover and leave to marinate in the refrigerator.

Heat the oil in a large, heavy-based saucepan over a medium heat, add the onion, celery and yellow pepper and cook gently for 12–15 minutes or until softened.

Add the preserved lemons, reserving 2 tablespoons for garnish. Stir in the cherry tomatoes, chickpeas, saffron and remaining chermoula and season to taste with salt and pepper. Stir-fry for 2–3 minutes and then pour over the stock. Bring to the boil, cover and simmer gently for 10 minutes.

Use a large spoon to remove half of the chickpea mixture from the pan. Lay the marinated fish over the remaining mixture in the pan, then return the chickpeas to the pan, covering the fish. Scatter over the olives, cover and simmer gently over a medium-low heat for 10 minutes or until the fish is cooked through.

Ladle the tagine into bowls and sprinkle with the reserved chopped lemon and coriander leaves. Serve with steamed wholewheat couscous.

For homemade chermoula, dry-fry 1 teaspoon each of cumin and coriander seeds in a frying pan until fragrant, tip into a spice grinder or mini chopper and grind to a powder. Add 1 teaspoon each of ground turmeric and ras el hanout, 2 roughly chopped garlic cloves, 1 small bunch each of parsley and coriander and 3 tablespoons lemon juice. Blend until smooth, then stir in 2 tablespoons olive oil. Store in an airtight container in the refrigerator for up to 2–3 days.

red fish curry

Serves **4**
Preparation time **15 minutes**
Cooking time **about**
10 minutes

1 tablespoon **groundnut oil**
1½–2 tablespoons **red**
  curry paste (see below
  for homemade)
200 ml (7 fl oz) **coconut**
  cream
250 ml (8 fl oz) **vegetable**
  stock
1 tablespoon **tamarind paste**
1 tablespoon **Thai fish sauce**
1 tablespoon **soft dark brown**
  sugar
200 g (7 oz) **broccoli florets**
200 g (7 oz) **green beans**,
  trimmed and cut into 2.5 cm
  (1 inch) lengths
450 g (14½ oz) thick **white**
  fish fillets, skinned, boned
  and cut into chunks
150 g (5 oz) can **bamboo**
  shoots, drained (optional)
small handful of **Thai basil** or
  coriander leaves, to garnish
lime wedges, to serve

Heat the oil in a wok or large frying pan over a medium heat, add the curry paste and stir-fry for 1–2 minutes. Stir in the coconut cream, stock, tamarind paste, fish sauce and sugar and bring to the boil, then reduce the heat and simmer gently for a further 2–3 minutes. Add the broccoli and beans and simmer gently for 2 minutes.

Stir in the fish and simmer gently for a further 3–4 minutes or until just cooked through. Stir in the bamboo shoots, if using.

Ladle into bowls, sprinkle with the Thai basil or coriander leaves and serve with lime wedges and boiled Thai brown rice.

For homemade red curry paste, put 2 roughly chopped garlic cloves, 2 roughly chopped shallots, 2–3 deseeded and roughly chopped red chillies, 2.5 cm (1 inch) piece of peeled and roughly chopped fresh root ginger, 1 chopped lemon grass stalk, 1 tablespoon Thai fish sauce, 1½ tablespoons palm sugar or soft light brown sugar, 3 shredded kaffir lime leaves or finely grated rind of 1 lime, 1 tablespoon lime juice, ½ teaspoon cumin seeds and ½ teaspoon coriander seeds in a small food processor and blend to a smooth paste. Store in an airtight container in the refrigerator for up to 1 week.

spicy tuna, tomato & olive pasta

Serves **4**
Preparation time **10 minutes**
Cooking time **10–12 minutes**

400 g (13 oz) **penne** or
  rigatoni
2 tablespoons **olive oil**, plus
  extra to serve
2 **garlic cloves**, thinly sliced
large pinch of **chilli flakes**
400 g (13 oz) **tomatoes**,
  roughly chopped
50 g (2 oz) **pitted black
  olives**, roughly chopped
1 tablespoon roughly chopped
  thyme
300 g (10 oz) can **tuna** in olive
  oil, drained
salt and **pepper**

Cook the pasta in a large saucepan of salted boiling water for 10–12 minutes, or according to the packet instructions, until al dente.

Meanwhile, heat the oil in a large frying pan over a medium heat and add the garlic, chilli flakes, tomatoes, olives and thyme. Bring to the boil, then reduce the heat and simmer for 5 minutes. Break the tuna up with a fork and stir into the sauce. Simmer for 2 minutes, then season with salt and pepper.

Drain the pasta, then toss into the sauce. Serve immediately, drizzled with extra olive oil.

For fresh tuna sauce, cut a 300 g (10 oz) tuna steak into strips and season with salt and pepper. Pan-fry in the olive oil for 2 minutes before adding the other ingredients and cooking for 5 minutes.

tuna steaks with wasabi dressing

Serves **4**
Preparation time **5 minutes**
Cooking time **6–7 minutes**

4 **tuna steaks**, about 150 g
   (5 oz) each
2 teaspoons **mixed
   peppercorns**, crushed
250 g (8 oz) **sugar snap peas**
1 teaspoon **toasted sesame
   oil**
2 teaspoons **sesame seeds**,
   lightly toasted

Dressing
2 tablespoons **light soy sauce**
4 tablespoons **mirin**
1 teaspoon **sugar**
1 teaspoon **wasabi paste**

Season the tuna steaks with the crushed peppercorns. Heat a griddle pan over a medium-high heat and griddle the tuna steaks for 2 minutes on each side until browned but still pink in the centre. Remove from the pan and leave to rest.

Put the sugar snap peas in a steamer basket and lower into a shallow saucepan of boiling water so that the peas are not quite touching the water. Drizzle with the sesame oil, cover and steam for 2–3 minutes or until tender. Alternatively, cook the peas in a bamboo or electric steamer.

Place all of the dressing ingredients in a screw-top jar and seal with a tight-fitting lid. Shake vigorously until well combined.

Divide the sugar snap peas between 4 serving dishes, then cut the tuna steaks in half diagonally and arrange over the peas. Drizzle with the prepared dressing and sprinkle with the sesame seeds. Serve immediately, with cellophane rice noodles, if liked.

For tuna carpaccio, roll 500 g (1 lb) tuna fillet in the peppercorns and seal on all sides in a very hot frying pan. Cool, wrap in clingfilm and place in the freezer for 1 hour until semi-frozen. Remove and cut into very thin slices. Arrange the slices on large plates and drizzle with the dressing. Serve with the steamed and chilled sugar snap peas, scattered with sesame seeds.

pot-roasted tuna with lentils

Serves **4**
Preparation time **15 minutes**
Cooking time **50 minutes–
 1 hour 10 minutes**

½ teaspoon **celery salt**
750 g (1 ½ lb) **tuna**, in one
 slender piece
3 tablespoons **olive oil**
1 **fennel bulb**, thinly sliced
250 g (8 oz) **black lentils**,
 rinsed
1 glass **white wine**, about
 150ml (¼ pint)
250 ml (8 fl oz) **fish** or
 vegetable stock
4 tablespoons chopped **fennel
 leaves** or **dill**
2 tablespoons **capers**, rinsed
 and drained
400 g (13 oz) can **chopped
 tomatoes**
salt and **pepper**

Mix the celery salt with a little pepper and rub all over
the tuna. Heat the oil in a flameproof casserole over
a medium-high heat and fry the tuna on all sides until
browned. Remove with a slotted spoon and drain on
kitchen paper on a plate. Add the sliced fennel to the
pan and fry gently until softened.

Stir in the lentils and wine and bring to the boil, then
cook until the wine has reduced by about half. Stir in
the stock, fennel leaves or dill, capers and tomatoes
and bring to the boil. Cover and transfer to a preheated
oven, 180°C (350°F), Gas Mark 4, and cook for
15 minutes.

Add the tuna, return to the oven and cook for a further
20 minutes or until the lentils are completely tender
and the tuna is still slightly pink in the centre. If you
prefer it well done, return to the oven for a further
15–20 minutes. Season to taste with salt and pepper
and serve.

For pot-roasted lamb with lentils, replace the tuna
with a 625 g (1 ¼ lb) piece of rolled loin of lamb. Omit
the fennel bulb and celery salt and fry the lamb in the
oil as above. Cook the lentils as above, replacing the
fish or vegetable stock with 250 ml (8 fl oz) chicken
stock and the fennel leaves or dill with 4 tablespoons
chopped rosemary or oregano. Add the lamb and return
to the oven for a further 30 minutes. If you prefer your
lamb well done, cook for a further 20 minutes.

spicy monkfish & potato bake

Serves **4**
Preparation time **15 minutes**
Cooking time **about 1 hour
10 minutes**

2 tablespoons **olive oil**
1 large **red onion**, finely sliced
2 **garlic cloves**, 1 chopped
  and 1 crushed
1 teaspoon **turmeric**
1 teaspoon **hot smoked
  paprika**
1 teaspoon **ground cumin**
½ teaspoon **ground ginger**
2 tablespoons **tomato purée**
1 tablespoon **lemon juice**
875 g (1¾ lb) large **potatoes**,
  peeled and thinly sliced
500 g (1 lb) **monkfish tail**,
  cut into 4 pieces
250 g (8 oz) **roasted
  peppers**, thinly sliced
1 **preserved lemon**, finely
  chopped
450 ml (¾ pint) hot **fish** or
  vegetable stock
½ teaspoon **powdered
  saffron**
salt and **pepper**

Heat 1 tablespoon of the oil in a small frying pan over a medium heat, add the onion and chopped garlic and fry gently for 10 minutes or until softened.

Meanwhile, mix together all the spices with a little salt and pepper, the tomato purée, lemon juice, crushed garlic and remaining oil in a non-metallic dish. Put the potatoes in a large bowl and add all but 1½ tablespoons of the paste. Mix together to coat the potatoes. Rub the remaining paste over the monkfish, cover and leave to marinate in the refrigerator.

Stir the cooked onion, peppers and preserved lemon into the potatoes and tip into a large, shallow ovenproof dish. Pour over enough stock to almost cover the potatoes and place in a preheated oven, 180°C (350°F), Gas Mark 4, for 45 minutes or until the potatoes are almost tender.

Arrange the monkfish over the potatoes, adding a little more stock if necessary. Sprinkle over the saffron and return to the oven for a further 10–15 minutes or until the fish is just cooked through. Serve immediately.

For Malaysian-style monkfish, cook 2 tablespoons red curry paste in 1 tablespoon groundnut oil in a large frying pan. Add the onion and cook for about 5 minutes. Stir in 3 shredded kaffir lime leaves, 200 ml (7 fl oz) reduced-fat coconut milk, 200 ml (7 fl oz) fish or vegetable stock, 1 tablespoon fish sauce and 1 tablespoon light soy sauce. Bring to the boil, then tip into a shallow ovenproof dish with 500 g (1lb) cubed monkfish tail and bake in the oven for 20 minutes or until the fish is cooked through. Serve with steamed rice.

monkfish & sweet potato curry

Serves **4**

Preparation time **15 minutes**

Cooking time **about
20 minutes**

2 **lemon grass stalks**, roughly
chopped

2 **shallots**, roughly chopped

1 large **red chilli**, deseeded

1 **garlic clove**

1.5 cm (¾ inch) piece of **fresh
root ginger**, peeled and
chopped

3 tablespoons **groundnut oil**

2 x 400 ml (14 fl oz) cans
reduced-fat coconut milk

2 **sweet potatoes,** cut into
1.5cm (¾ inch) cubes

2 large **monkfish tails,** about
250 g (8 oz) each, cut into
large chunks

2 tablespoons **Thai fish sauce**

1 teaspoon **soft dark brown
sugar**

1 ½ tablespoons **lime juice**

2 tablespoons roughly
chopped **coriander**,
to garnish

Put the lemon grass, shallots, chilli, garlic, ginger and
oil in a food processor or blender and blend to a
smooth paste.

Heat a saucepan over a medium heat, add the paste
and fry for 2 minutes until fragrant, then add the
coconut milk. Bring to the boil and cook for 5 minutes
until it reaches the consistency of cream. Add the sweet
potatoes and cook until almost tender.

Add the monkfish and simmer for a further 5 minutes
or until the fish is firm and cooked through. Add the fish
sauce, sugar and lime juice, to taste. Sprinkle with the
coriander and serve with some Thai sticky rice.

For Thai-roasted monkfish with roasted chilli
pumpkin, mix 2 tablespoons Thai red curry paste with
4 tablespoons fat-free natural yogurt in a non-metallic
bowl. Add 2 monkfish tails, cut into large pieces, cover
and leave to marinate in the refrigerator for at least
20 minutes or overnight if possible. Pan-fry the pieces
of fish in a little vegetable oil until cooked through. Cut
a 500 g (1 lb) pumpkin in half, scoop out the seeds,
peel and cut into 2.5 cm (1 inch) cubes. Sprinkle with
dried chilli flakes and roast in a preheated oven, 200°C
(400°F), Gas Mark 6, for 15–20 minutes, or until
tender, turning occasionally, . Serve with extra natural
yogurt mixed with chopped coriander.

monkfish with winter vegetables

Serves **4**
Preparation time **20 minutes**
Cooking time **about**
  40 minutes

2 tablespoons **olive oil**
25 g (1 oz) **butter**
1 **red onion**, chopped
2 **garlic cloves**, chopped
325 g (11 oz) **parsnips**,
  peeled and diced
375 g (12 oz) **swedes**, peeled
  and diced
375 g (12 oz) **turnips**, peeled
  and diced
300 g (10 oz) **carrots**, peeled
  and diced
1 teaspoon chopped **thyme**
1 tablespoon chopped **sage**
1 teaspoon chopped **dill**
1 tablespoon chopped
  oregano or 1 teaspoon
  dried oregano
2 **bay leaves**
500 g (1 lb) **monkfish tail**,
  cubed
150 ml (¼ pint) **white wine**
150 ml (¼ pint) **vegetable**
  stock
salt and **pepper**

Heat the oil and butter in a large, heavy-based saucepan over a medium heat, add the onion and garlic and fry for 8–9 minutes or until softened and lightly golden. Add the remaining vegetables and the herbs and stir for 10 minutes or until lightly golden. Remove with a slotted spoon and set aside.

Increase the heat to medium-high, add the monkfish and season with salt and pepper. Fry for 3–4 minutes, stirring occasionally, or until lightly coloured all over. It may be necessary to add an extra teaspoon of oil.

Return the vegetables to the pan, then pour over the wine and stock and stir gently. Bring to the boil, then reduce the heat, cover and simmer gently for 8–10 minutes or until the fish is cooked through and the vegetables are tender. Serve with steamed curly kale and crusty brown bread.

For monkfish in red wine, make as above, replacing the dill with 1 tablespoon chopped rosemary and the white wine and vegetable stock with 300 ml (½ pint) red wine and a 400 g (13 oz) can chopped tomatoes.

monkfish with coconut rice

Serves **4**
Preparation time **20 minutes**
Cooking time **25–30 minutes**

4 long, slender **lemon grass
    stalks**
625 g (1¼ lb) **monkfish
    fillets**, cut into 3 cm
    (1¼ inch) cubes
3 tablespoons **stir-fry** or **wok
    oil**
½ teaspoon crushed **chilli
    flakes**
2 **garlic cloves**, sliced
1 bunch of **spring onions**,
    finely chopped, white and
    green parts separate
300 g (10 oz) **Thai fragrant
    rice**
400 ml (14 fl oz) can **reduced-
    fat coconut milk**
50 g (2 oz) **creamed coconut**,
    chopped
200 ml (7 fl oz) **hot water**
2 tablespoons **rice wine
    vinegar**
150 g (5 oz) **baby leaf
    spinach**
salt and **pepper**

Using a large knife, slice each lemon grass stalk in half lengthways. (If the stalks are very thick, pull off the outer layers, finely chop them and add to the oil with the chilli flakes.) Cut the thin ends of each stalk to a point and thread the monkfish on to the skewers. If it is difficult to thread the fish, pierce each piece with a small knife first to make threading easier.

Heat the oil with the chilli flakes, garlic and white parts of the spring onions in a large frying pan over a medium heat. Add the monkfish skewers and fry gently for about 5 minutes, turning once, until cooked through. Remove from the pan, drain on a plate and keep warm.

Add the rice, coconut milk and creamed coconut to the pan, season with salt and pepper to taste and bring to the boil. Reduce the heat, cover with a lid or foil and cook gently for 6–8 minutes, stirring frequently, until the rice is almost tender and the milk absorbed. Add the measurement water and cook, covered, for a further 10 minutes or until the rice is completely tender, adding a little more water if the mixture boils dry before the rice is tender.

Stir in the vinegar, remaining spring onions and spinach, turning it in the rice until wilted. Arrange the skewers over the rice. Cover and cook gently for 3 minutes, then serve immediately.

poached sea bass & salsa

Serves **4**
Preparation time **15 minutes**
Cooking time **25 minutes**

5 cm (2 inch) piece of **fresh
    root ginger**, peeled and
    thinly sliced
2 **lemon grass stalks**, sliced
    lengthways
1 **lime**, sliced
200 ml (7 fl oz) **dry sherry**
2 tablespoons **fish sauce**
2 **sea bass**, about 625 g
    (1 ¼ lb) each, cleaned and
    scaled

Salsa

3 firm **tomatoes**, deseeded
    and finely diced
1 **lemon grass stalk**, tough
    outer leaves discarded, finely
    chopped
1 teaspoon peeled and finely
    grated **fresh root ginger**
2 tablespoons chopped
    coriander
2 **spring onions**, finely
    chopped
2 teaspoons **groundnut oil**
1 tablespoon **lime juice**
1 ½ teaspoons **light soy
    sauce**

Put the ginger, lemon grass, lime, sherry, fish sauce and
enough water to just cover the fish in a fish kettle or
large frying pan. Bring to the boil, then reduce the heat
and simmer gently for 5 minutes.

Place the sea bass in the fish kettle or on a large piece
of nonstick baking paper if using a frying pan. Lower
into the stock, adding more water if necessary so that it
covers the fish. Bring the stock to the boil and then turn
off the heat. Cover and leave to poach for 15 minutes
or until the fish flakes easily when pressed in the centre
with a knife.

Meanwhile, make the salsa. Place the tomatoes, lemon
grass, ginger, coriander and spring onions in a bowl.
Stir through the oil, lime juice and soy sauce and leave
to infuse.

Lift the poached sea bass carefully from the cooking
liquid on to a plate. Peel away the skin and gently lift
the fillets from the bones. Place on a serving dish with
the salsa and serve with steamed rice and lime wedges,
if liked.

For pan-fried sea bass with salsa, ask the
fishmonger to fillet the whole sea bass. Heat
1 tablespoon olive oil in a nonstick frying pan and
pan-fry the sea bass fillets over a medium-high heat,
skin side down, for 3–4 minutes. Reduce the heat,
cover and cook for a further 3–4 minutes or until
cooked through. Serve with the salsa.

plaice with vegetables provençale

Serves **4**
Preparation time **15 minutes**
Cooking time **45–50 minutes**

2 **courgettes**, sliced
1 **aubergine**, sliced
4 **tomatoes**, quartered
1 **onion**, thickly sliced
1 large **red pepper**, cored,
   deseeded and sliced
3 **garlic cloves**, sliced
1 small bunch of **basil**,
   chopped, plus extra
   shredded leaves to garnish
1 tablespoon chopped **thyme**
3 tablespoons chopped
   parsley
olive oil spray
3 tablespoons **plain flour**
4 **plaice fillets**, about 150 g
   (5 oz) each
1½ tablespoons **olive oil**
salt and **pepper**

Mix all the vegetables and the chopped herbs in a large roasting tin and season with salt and pepper. Spray with a little olive oil and place in a preheated oven, 180°C (350°F), Gas Mark 4, for 40–45 minutes or until the vegetables are tender.

Put the flour on a plate and season with salt and pepper, then dust the plaice fillets in the flour. Heat the oil in a large, nonstick frying pan over a medium heat, add the fish, skin side down, and fry for 2–3 minutes, then turn the fish over using a fish slice and cook for a further 2–3 minutes or until golden. The flesh should be white and flake easily when pressed in the centre with a knife.

Spoon the vegetables on to serving plates and top with the plaice fillets. Serve immediately, garnished with the shredded basil.

For vegetable provençale bake, slice all the vegetables and arrange in a shallow ovenproof dish. Season with salt and pepper, drizzle with the olive oil and pour over 500 ml (17 fl oz) passata. Sprinkle with the chopped herbs and 2 tablespoons grated Parmesan cheese. Place in the preheated oven for 45 minutes or until the vegetables are tender. Serve with a green salad and crusty bread.

feta-stuffed plaice

Serves **4**
Preparation time **20 minutes**
Cooking time **40 minutes**

2 tablespoons chopped **mint**
2 tablespoons chopped
    oregano
25 g (1 oz) **Parma ham**, finely
    chopped
2 **garlic cloves**, finely chopped
4 **spring onions**, finely
    chopped
200 g (7 oz) **reduced-fat feta
    cheese**
8 **plaice fillets**, skinned
300 g (10 oz) **courgettes**,
    sliced
4 tablespoons **garlic-infused
    olive oil**
8 **flat mushrooms**
150 g (5 oz) **baby plum
    tomatoes**, halved
1 tablespoon **capers**, rinsed
    and drained
salt and **pepper**

Put the mint, oregano, ham, garlic and spring onions in a bowl. Crumble in the feta cheese, season with plenty of pepper and mix together well.

Put the fish fillets, skin side up, on a clean work surface and press the feta mixture down the centres. Roll up loosely and secure with wooden cocktail sticks.

Scatter the courgettes into a shallow, ovenproof dish and drizzle with 1 tablespoon of the oil. Place in a preheated oven, 190°C (375°F), Gas Mark 5, for 15 minutes. Add the plaice fillets to the dish. Tuck the mushrooms, tomatoes and capers around the fish and season lightly with salt and pepper. Drizzle with the remaining oil.

Return to the oven for a further 25 minutes or until the fish is cooked through. Serve with tomato and garlic bread (see below).

For tomato & garlic bread, to serve as an accompaniment, mix together 75 g (3 oz) softened butter, 2 crushed garlic cloves, 3 tablespoons sun-dried tomato paste and a little salt and pepper. Make vertical cuts 2.5 cm (1 inch) apart through a ciabatta loaf, cutting not quite through the base. Push the garlic and tomato paste mixture into the cuts. Wrap in foil and bake in the oven on the tray beneath the fish for 15 minutes, then open up the foil and return the bread to the oven for 10 minutes.

pollack with puy lentils & fennel

Serves **4**
Preparation time **12 minutes**
Cooking time **about
    25 minutes**

2 **fennel bulbs,** thinly sliced
1.8 litres (3 pints) **vegetable
    stock**
250 g (8 oz) **Puy lentils,**
    rinsed
1½ tablespoons **olive oil**
1 **onion,** chopped
1 **garlic clove,** chopped
50 g (2 oz) **sun-dried
    tomatoes** (not in oil),
    chopped
1 small bunch of **parsley,**
    chopped, plus extra to
    garnish
finely grated rind and juice of
    1 lemon
4 thick **pollack fillets,** about
    150 g (5 oz) each
2 teaspoons **capers,** rinsed,
    drained and chopped
4 large, slices of lean **Parma
    ham**
salt and **pepper**

Arrange the fennel over the base of a large ovenproof
dish. Pour over 200 ml (7 fl oz) of the stock to just cover
the slices. Season with salt and pepper and place in a
preheated oven, 180°C (350°F), Gas Mark 4, for about
25 minutes or until softened.

Meanwhile, put the remaining stock and lentils in a
large saucepan and bring to the boil. Reduce the heat
and simmer for 20 minutes or until tender. Drain the
lentils, reserving 200 ml (7 fl oz) of the cooking liquid.

Heat 1 tablespoon of the oil in another saucepan over a
medium heat, add the onion and fry for 7–8 minutes or
until softened. Add the garlic and cook for a further
2–3 minutes. Stir the drained lentils into the onions with
the reserved cooking liquid and the sun-dried tomatoes
and simmer for 1–2 minutes. Stir in the parsley and
lemon juice and season to taste.

Towards the end of the fennel and lentil cooking time,
sprinkle each pollack fillet with a little of the lemon
rind and capers. Season with pepper, then wrap each
fillet in a slice of Parma ham. Heat the remaining oil
in a large, nonstick frying pan over a medium high-
heat, add the pollack fillets and cook for 6–8 minutes,
turning occasionally, until the fish is cooked through and
the Parma ham crisp. Remove from the pan, drain on
kitchen paper and rest for 2–3 minutes.

Spoon the lentils into dishes and top with the fennel.
Slice the fish in half diagonally and arrange over the
fennel. Serve immediately with extra chopped parsley
sprinkled over.

clam & tomato spaghetti

Serves **4**
Preparation time **10 minutes**
Cooking time **20–25 minutes**

2 tablespoons **olive oil**
1 **onion**, sliced
2 **garlic cloves**, finely chopped
1 **red chilli**, deseeded and
    finely chopped (optional)
250 g (8 oz) **cherry tomatoes**,
    quartered
125 ml (4 fl oz) **dry white
    wine**
2–3 tablespoons chopped
    parsley
1 kg (2 lb) **live clams**, cleaned
    (discard any that don't shut
    when tapped)
400 g (13 oz) **wholemeal
    spaghetti**
1½ tablespoons **truffle oil**
salt and **pepper**

Heat the olive oil in a large saucepan over a low heat, add the onion and garlic and cook for 12–15 minutes or until softened. Add the chilli, if using, tomatoes, white wine and parsley and season with salt and pepper. Bring to the boil, then reduce the heat and simmer for 2–3 minutes.

Add the clams, cover with a tight-fitting lid and cook gently for 4–5 minutes or until they have opened. Discard any clams that remain closed.

Meanwhile, cook the spaghetti in a large saucepan of salted boiling water for 10–12 minutes, or according to the packet instructions, until al dente. Drain well and place in a serving dish.

Heap the clam and tomato sauce over the spaghetti, drizzle with the truffle oil and sprinkle with pepper. Serve immediately with crusty bread.

For mixed seafood fettucine, replace the spaghetti with 400 g (13 oz) fettucine and cook the pasta as above. Make the tomato sauce as above, leaving it to simmer for 10 minutes after adding the wine. Omit the live clams and stir through 400 g (13 oz) raw peeled fruits de mer or seafood selection, and cook for 5 minutes or until the seafood is cooked through and piping hot. Serve with the fettucine as above, drizzled with basil or chilli oil.

scallops with spiced lentils

Serves **4**
Preparation time **10 minutes**
Cooking time **20–25 minutes**

250 g (8 oz) **red lentils**, rinsed
5 tablespoons **olive oil**
25 g (1 oz) **butter**
1 **onion**, finely chopped
1 **aubergine**, cut into 1 cm
   (½ inch) cubes
1 **garlic clove**, finely chopped
1 tablespoon **curry powder**
1 tablespoon chopped
   parsley, plus extra to garnish
12 cleaned **king scallops**,
   corals removed (optional)
4 tablespoons **fat-free Greek
   yogurt**
salt and **pepper**

Cook the lentils in a saucepan of boiling water according to the packet instructions. Drain well.

Meanwhile, heat 1 tablespoon of the oil and the butter in a frying pan over a medium heat, add the onion and cook slowly for 10 minutes or until golden brown. Remove with a slotted spoon to a plate and turn the heat up to high. Add another 2 tablespoons of the oil to the pan and fry the aubergine in batches until coloured and softened.

Return the onion to the pan with the garlic, curry powder and cooked lentils and fry for a further minute to warm through. Season with salt and pepper and stir in the parsley.

Heat a frying pan over a high heat, then add the remaining 2 tablespoons of oil. Season the scallops with salt and pepper, place them in the frying pan and cook for 1 minute on each side or until just cooked through. Serve the scallops immediately with the spiced lentils and Greek yogurt, garnished with parsley leaves.

For scallops with dhal & spinach, cook 250 g (8 oz) yellow split pea lentils according to the packet instructions and drain well. Heat a little vegetable oil in a frying pan, add the onion and garlic, omitting the aubergine, and fry until softened. Add 1 teaspoon curry powder, 1 teaspoon garam masala and a pinch of turmeric and fry for 1 minute. Add the cooked lentils with a little water or chicken stock to moisten the mixture. Add 500 g (1 lb) baby leaf spinach and stir until wilted. Cook the scallops as above with a light sprinkle of curry powder on each. Serve with the dhal.

prawn & soba noodle salad

Serves **4**

Preparation time **10 minutes**,
  plus cooling

Cooking time **about
  10 minutes**

400 g (13 oz) **raw peeled
  prawns**

finely grated rind of 1 **lime**

1 tablespoon peeled and finely
  shredded **fresh root ginger**

1 **red chilli**, deseeded and
  finely chopped

400 g (13 oz) **soba noodles**

2 **spring onions**, thinly sliced

Dressing

juice of 1 **lime**

1 tablespoon **soft dark brown
  sugar**

2 tablespoons **mirin**

2 tablespoons **fish sauce**

1 small bunch of **coriander**,
  chopped

1 small bunch of **mint**,
  chopped

Mix together the prawns, lime rind, ginger and chilli in a bowl. Tip into a steamer basket and lower into a shallow saucepan of boiling water so the prawns are not quite touching the water. Cover and steam for 3–4 minutes or until the prawns turn pink and are cooked through. Alternatively, cook the prawns in a bamboo or electric steamer. Remove from the pan and leave to cool.

Meanwhile, whisk together all the dressing ingredients in a small bowl.

Cook the noodles in a large saucepan of boiling water for 6–7 minutes, or according to the packet instructions, until tender. Drain well and rinse under running cold water. Toss with the dressing.

Divide the noodles between 4 bowls, scatter over the spring onions and prawns and serve immediately.

For aromatic prawn stir-fry, heat 2 teaspoons groundnut oil in a hot wok or large frying pan and stir-fry the marinated prawns until they turn pink and are just cooked through. Add the drained noodles and toss to reheat. Drizzle over the dressing and serve immediately, sprinkled with the spring onions.

mussels with bacon

Serves **4**
Preparation time **8 minutes**
Cooking time **30–35 minutes**

6 lean **back bacon rashers**,
  chopped
2 **shallots**, sliced
2 **garlic cloves**, chopped
250 ml (8 fl oz) **white wine**
400 g (13 oz) can **chopped
  tomatoes**
1 tablespoon chopped **thyme**,
  plus extra sprigs to garnish
2 kg (4 lb) **live mussels**,
  scrubbed and debearded
  (discard any that don't shut
  when tapped)
2–3 tablespoons **half-fat
  crème fraîche** (optional)
salt and **pepper**

Heat a very large, heavy-based saucepan over a medium heat, then add the bacon and dry-fry for 3–4 minutes or until beginning to colour. If the bacon is very lean, fry in 1 tablespoon olive oil. Add the shallots and garlic and fry for 2–3 minutes or until softened.

Stir in the white wine, tomatoes and thyme and season with salt and pepper to taste. Bring to the boil, then reduce the heat and simmer for 20 minutes or until the sauce has thickened.

Add the mussels and stir to coat, then cover with a tight-fitting lid and cook for 4–5 minutes, or until the mussels have opened, stirring once. Discard any that remain closed.

Stir in the crème fraîche, if using, and serve in deep bowls garnished with thyme sprigs.

For traditional moules marinières, omit the bacon and cook the shallots and garlic in a knob of butter. Pour in the white wine, or replace with 250 ml (8 fl oz) dry cider, and then add the mussels. Cook as above. Stir in the crème fraîche and scatter with chopped parsley to serve.

peanut, squid & noodle salad

Serves **4**
Preparation time **25 minutes**,
  plus standing
Cooking time **15 minutes**

175 g (6 oz) **thin rice noodles**
500 g (1 lb) prepared **baby
  squid**, cleaned
3 **red chillies**, deseeded and
  finely chopped
3 **garlic cloves**, finely chopped
2 tablespoons chopped
  coriander, plus extra leaves
  to garnish
3 tablespoons **groundnut oil**
175 g (6 oz) **unsalted
  peanuts**, roughly chopped
125 g (4 oz) **green beans**,
  trimmed and shredded
3 tablespoons **Thai fish sauce**
1 teaspoon **caster sugar**
3 tablespoons **lemon juice**
lime wedges, to serve
  (optional)

Put the noodles in a large heatproof bowl, pour over boiling water to cover and leave to stand for 5–8 minutes, or according to the packet instructions, until tender. Drain well and rinse in cold water.

Cut the squid bodies in half lengthways and use a sharp knife to make a series of slashes in a diagonal criss-cross pattern on the underside of each piece.

Mix together the chillies, garlic and chopped coriander in a non-metallic bowl. Add the squid pieces and toss in the mixture, then leave to stand for about 20 minutes.

Heat the oil in a wok or large frying pan over a medium heat and toast the peanuts for 2–3 minutes or until golden brown. Remove with a slotted spoon and set aside. Add the squid to the wok or pan and stir-fry for 2–3 minutes or until the squid have begun to curl and turn white. Set aside with the peanuts.

Add the beans to the wok or pan and stir-fry for 2 minutes. Stir in the fish sauce, sugar, lemon juice and 3 tablespoons water and cook for a further 1 minute. Remove the pan from the heat, add the drained noodles and toss together. Add the peanuts, squid and extra coriander leaves and toss again. Serve warm or cool with lime wedges, if liked.

meat & poultry

gingery pork chops

Serves **4**
Preparation time **15 minutes**
Cooking time **20 minutes**

4 lean **pork chops**, about
    150 g (5 oz) each
3.5 cm (1½ inch) piece of
    fresh root ginger, peeled
    and grated
1 teaspoon **sesame oil**
1 tablespoon **dark soy sauce**
2 teaspoons **stem ginger**
    syrup or **runny honey**

Dressing
1½ tablespoons **light soy**
    sauce
juice of 1 **blood orange**
2 pieces of **stem ginger**, finely
    chopped

Salad
2 large **carrots**, peeled and
    coarsely grated
150 g (5 oz) **mangetout**,
    shredded
100 g (3½ oz) **bean sprouts**
2 **spring onions**, thinly sliced
2 tablespoons **unsalted**
    peanuts, roughly chopped
    (optional)

Place the pork in a shallow ovenproof dish and rub
with the ginger, sesame oil, soy sauce and stem ginger
syrup or honey until well covered. Leave to marinate for
10 minutes.

Make the dressing. Mix together all the ingredients in a
bowl and set aside for the flavours to develop.

Cook the pork in a preheated oven, 180°C (350°F),
Gas Mark 4, for 18–20 minutes or until cooked through
but still juicy.

Meanwhile, mix the carrots, mangetout, bean sprouts
and spring onions in a large bowl. Just before serving,
toss with the dressing and pile into serving dishes.
Sprinkle with the peanuts, if using, and top with
the pork chops, drizzled with cooking juices. Serve
immediately with steamed rice.

For pork & ginger stir-fry, replace the pork chops
with 4 lean boneless pork loin steaks and thinly slice.
Cut the carrots into matchsticks. Heat 1–2 teaspoons
sesame oil in a hot wok or large frying pan, add the
pork and stir-fry until just cooked. Add the carrots,
mangetout, bean sprouts and spring onions and stir-fry
for a further 1–2 minutes. Toss with the dressing and
serve immediately, sprinkled with the peanuts, if liked.

soy & sake pork with pak choi

Serves **4**
Preparation time **5 minutes**
Cooking time **15–20 minutes**

100 ml (3½ fl oz) **Japanese
  soy sauce**
100 ml (3½ fl oz) **sake**
1½ tablespoons **sugar**
500 g (1 lb) lean **pork loin** or
  fillet, cut into 2.5 cm (1 inch)
  cubes
750 g (1½ lb) **pak choi**, cut in
  half lengthways
sesame seeds, to garnish

Put the soy sauce, sake and sugar in a large, deep frying pan and stir to dissolve the sugar. Bring to the boil and simmer for 3–4 minutes. Add the pork and simmer gently for 7–8 minutes, or until the pork is just cooked through, turning occasionally. Remove from the heat and leave to rest.

Place the pak choi in a steamer basket and lower into a shallow saucepan of boiling water so that the pak choi is not quite touching the water. Cover and steam for 3–4 minutes or until tender. Alternatively, use a bamboo or electric steamer.

Arrange the pak choi in serving dishes with the pork and its cooking liquid and steamed Thai jasmine rice. Sprinkle over sesame seeds and serve immediately.

For Japanese tofu & vegetables, make as above, replacing the pork with 500 g (1 lb) firm, sliced or cubed tofu and the pak choi with 250 g (8 oz) green beans and 500 g (1 lb) mixed Asian-style vegetables.

pork & broccoli noodles

Serves **4**
Preparation time **10 minutes**
Cooking time **about**
   20 minutes

2 tablespoons **light soy sauce**
1 teaspoon **fish sauce**
2 tablespoons **oyster sauce**
500 g (1 lb) **pork tenderloin
fillet**
1 tablespoon **groundnut oil**
2 large **eggs**, lightly beaten
2 **spring onions**, finely sliced
400 g (13 oz) **purple
sprouting broccoli spears**
400 g (13 oz) **thick rice
noodles**

Mix together the soy sauce, fish sauce and oyster sauce in a bowl. Rub half of the sauce over the pork and place in a small, nonstick roasting tin. Place in a preheated oven, 180°C (350°F), Gas Mark 4, for about 20 minutes or until cooked through but still juicy. Leave to rest for 5–10 minutes.

Meanwhile, heat the oil in a smoking hot wok or large frying pan and pour in the beaten eggs, swirling to cover the hot surface. Scatter over the sliced spring onions and cook for 1–2 minutes or until the egg is set and beginning to colour. Remove and slice thinly.

Put the broccoli in a steamer basket and lower into a shallow saucepan of boiling water so that the spears are not quite touching the water. Cover and steam for 3–4 minutes or until just tender. Alternatively, use a bamboo or electric steamer.

Cook the noodles in a large saucepan of boiling water for 3–4 minutes, or according to the packet instructions, until tender. Drain and heap on to serving plates.

Toss the broccoli in the remaining sauce mixture, spoon on to the noodles and scatter with the sliced omelette. Slice the pork and arrange over the noodles. Drizzle with any cooking juices and serve immediately.

For quick pork stir-fry, make the omelette as above and set aside. Reheat the wok or frying pan and stir-fry the thinly sliced pork fillet until almost cooked through. Add the broccoli spears, cook for a further 2–3 minutes, then pour over the sauce. Serve immediately with boiled rice or egg noodles and the sliced omelette.

lamb skewers with turkish salad

Serves **4**
Preparation time **20 minutes**
Cooking time **5–10 minutes**

750 g (1½ lb) **lamb fillet**,
    trimmed and cubed
1 teaspoon **olive oil**
1 teaspoon **dried oregano**
finely grated rind of 1 **lemon**
½ teaspoon **ground paprika**
4 wholemeal **pitta breads**
salt and **pepper**
lemon wedges, to serve
    (optional)

Turkish salad
1 small **cucumber**, deseeded
    and chopped
4 firm, ripe **tomatoes**,
    deseeded and chopped
1 **green pepper**, cored,
    deseeded and chopped
1 small **red onion**, chopped
1 small bunch of **mint**, finely
    chopped
1 tablespoon **extra virgin
    rapeseed** or **olive oil**
100 g (3½ oz) **reduced-fat
    feta cheese**, diced
2 tablespoons chopped
    parsley
juice of 1 **lemon**

Rub the lamb with the olive oil, dried oregano, lemon rind, paprika and salt and pepper. Thread on to 4 long or 8 short metal skewers and leave to marinate for at least 10 minutes.

Make the salad. Mix together the cucumber, tomatoes, green pepper, onion, mint and rapeseed or olive oil in a large serving bowl and sprinkle over the feta and parsley. Stir in the lemon juice and season well with salt and pepper. Set aside.

Cook the lamb skewers under a preheated hot grill or on the barbecue for 5–10 minutes, or until cooked to the pinkness desired, turning occasionally. Remove from the grill and leave to rest for 2–3 minutes.

Meanwhile, wrap the pitta breads in foil and place in a preheated oven, 180°C (350°F), Gas Mark 4, for 5–8 minutes or until warm. Arrange the lamb skewers on the pitta breads with the Turkish salad. Serve with lemon wedges and griddled aubergines, if liked (see below).

For griddled aubergines, to serve as an accompaniment, cut 2 medium aubergines into 5 mm (¼ inch) slices. Preheat a ridged griddle pan over a medium-high heat, add the aubergine slices in batches and cook for 4–5 minutes, turning once, until charred and tender. Place in a serving dish, season with a little salt and pepper and drizzle with extra virgin rapeseed oil.

japanese beef noodles

Serves **4**
Preparation time **10 minutes**,
  plus freezing
Cooking time **8 minutes**

400 g (13 oz) thin **beef fillet**
3 tablespoons **Japanese soy
  sauce**
3 tablespoons **mirin**
3 tablespoons **sake**
1½ teaspoons **sugar**
400 g (13 oz) **brown udon
  noodles**
1 tablespoon **toasted sesame
  oil**
2 **onions**, sliced
200 g (7 oz) **shiitake** or
  chestnut mushrooms,
  sliced
160 g (5½ oz) **bean sprouts**
  or **enoki mushrooms**
1 **spring onion**, thinly sliced
2 teaspoons **sesame seeds**

Wrap the beef fillet in clingfilm and place in the freezer for about 1 hour until it is semi-frozen. Remove and use a sharp knife to slice very thinly, against the grain.

Whisk together the soy sauce, mirin, sake and sugar in a small bowl to make a sauce.

Cook the noodles in a large saucepan of boiling water for 6–8 minutes, or according to the packet instructions, until tender.

Meanwhile, heat a wok or large frying pan until smoking hot, add the sesame oil and onions and stir-fry for 2–3 minutes. Add the shiitake or chestnut mushrooms and the bean sprouts or enoki mushrooms and stir-fry for a further 2–3 minutes or until softened. Stir in the beef and fry for 2 minutes, then pour in the prepared sauce and bubble for 1 minute.

Drain the noodles and heap into deep bowls, then spoon over the beef, pouring over any sauce left in the wok. Sprinkle with the spring onion and sesame seeds and serve immediately.

For tofu, mushroom & mangetout stir-fry, make the sauce and cook the noodles as above. Replace the beef with 400 g (13 oz) firm silken tofu, sliced. Stir-fry the onions and mushrooms as above, then add the tofu and 125 g (4 oz) mangetout and stir-fry for 2–3 minutes. Pour in the sauce and continue as above.

thai-style beef salad

Serves **4–6**
Preparation time **20 minutes**
Cooking time **10 minutes**

125 g (4 oz) **green papaya**,
  peeled and deseeded
125 g (4 oz) **green mango**,
  peeled and stoned
handful of **mint leaves**,
  chopped
handful of **Thai basil leaves**
2 small, elongated **shallots**,
  finely sliced
1 tablespoon **vegetable oil**
4 **sirloin steaks**, about 125 g
  (4 oz) each

Dressing
1 cm (½ inch) piece of **fresh
  root ginger**, peeled and
  finely sliced
1½ tablespoons **palm sugar**
  or **soft light brown sugar**
½ **red chilli**, deseeded and
  finely sliced
juice of 2 **limes**
2 tablespoons **Thai fish sauce**

Grate or slice the papaya and mango into long, thin strips. Put the papaya and mango, mint and basil leaves in a large salad bowl and mix together, then stir in the shallots.

Make the dressing. Crush the ginger and sugar using a pestle and mortar. Add the chilli, lime juice and fish sauce, to taste.

Heat a griddle pan over a high heat, add the oil and fry the steak for 5 minutes on each side or until cooked to the pinkness desired. Remove from the pan and leave to rest for 5 minutes.

Slice the steak diagonally into thin slices and arrange on serving plates. Add the dressing to the salad, mix well to combine and serve with the steak.

For toasted rice khao koor, a special garnish you can add to this salad, put 3 tablespoons raw jasmine rice in a small frying pan over a medium heat, stirring continuously, until all the rice is golden in colour. Allow the rice to cool, then grind it coarsely in a spice grinder or using a pestle and mortar, and sprinkle over the finished salad.

slow-cook beef curry

Serves **4–6**
Preparation time **20 minutes**
Cooking time **2¼ hours**

1 tablespoon **groundnut oil**
1 large **onion**, chopped
750 g (1½ lb) **stewing steak**, cubed
2 tablespoons **tomato purée**
3 **tomatoes**, chopped
3 tablespoons **fat-free natural yogurt**, plus extra to serve
1 teaspoon **black onion seeds**
salt and **pepper**

Curry paste
2 teaspoons **cumin seeds**
1 teaspoon **coriander seeds**
½ teaspoon **fennel seeds**
2 **garlic cloves**, chopped
1 tablespoon peeled and grated **fresh root ginger**
1–2 small **green chillies**, according to taste
1 teaspoon **ground paprika**
1 teaspoon **turmeric**
2 tablespoons **tomato purée**
2 tablespoons **groundnut oil**
25 g (1 oz) **coriander leaves**, plus extra to garnish

Make the curry paste. Place the whole spices in a small frying pan and dry-fry over a medium heat for 2–3 minutes, stirring frequently, until fragrant and beginning to pop. Grind to a powder in or mini chopper. Add to the remaining curry paste ingredients and blend to a smooth paste.

Heat the oil in a large, heavy-based saucepan over a medium heat, add the onion and cook for 5–6 minutes or until beginning to colour, stirring occasionally. Add 3 tablespoons of the prepared curry paste and stir-fry for 1–2 minutes to cook the spices.

Stir in the beef and cook for 4–5 minutes or until the meat is browned and well coated. Stir in the tomato purée, tomatoes and 250 ml (8 fl oz) water. Stir in the yogurt and bring to the boil, then reduce the heat, cover and simmer very gently for 2 hours or until tender, adding more liquid if necessary. Alternatively, cook in a slow cooker.

Season well with salt and pepper, then ladle into bowls. Spoon over extra yogurt and sprinkle with the black onion seeds and extra coriander. Serve hot with naan bread and steamed basmati rice, if liked.

For lamb curry with spinach & chickpeas, make the curry as above, replacing the curry paste with 4 tablespoons ready-made madras or rogan josh curry paste and the beef with 750 g (1½ lb) cubed lean leg of lamb. Stir a drained 400 g (13 oz) can chickpeas into the curry with the yogurt. Cook as above, stirring in 125 g (4 oz) baby leaf spinach at the end of the cooking time. Serve with naan bread and yogurt, if liked.

griddled beef & truffle polenta

Serves **4**
Preparation time **15 minutes**
Cooking time **15–20 minutes**

50 g (2 oz) **dried porcini
   mushrooms**, soaked in
   250ml (8 fl oz) boiling water
   for 10–15 minutes
7 teaspoons **olive oil**
1 **garlic clove**, chopped
800 ml (1½ pints) **hot beef**
   or **vegetable stock**
6 tablespoons chopped
   chives
4 **beef fillet steaks**, about
   175 g (6 oz) each
200 g (7 oz) **quick-cook
   polenta**
50 g (2 oz) **Parmesan
   cheese**, finely grated
2 teaspoons **truffle oil**
½ teaspoon **truffle salt**
   (optional)
handful of **rocket leaves**
salt and **pepper**

Drain the porcini, reserving the soaking liquid, then squeeze dry and roughly chop. Heat 3 teaspoons of the olive oil in a small frying pan over a medium heat, add the garlic and fry for 30 seconds. Add the mushrooms and fry for 1–2 minutes, then stir in 3 tablespoons of the reserved soaking liquid, 3 tablespoons of the stock and 1 tablespoon of the chives. Bubble for 1 minute, then remove from the heat and keep warm.

Rub 1 teaspoon of the remaining olive oil over each of the steaks, season with pepper and place on a preheated hot griddle pan. Cook for 2–5 minutes on each side until cooked to the pinkness desired. Remove and leave to rest for 4–5 minutes.

Pour the remaining mushroom soaking liquid and stock into a large saucepan and bring to the boil. Pour in the polenta in a steady stream, whisking gently until the polenta thickens, then reduce the heat and cook for 2 minutes. Stir in the Parmesan, truffle oil and 4 tablespoons of the chives. Season to taste.

Spoon the polenta onto serving plates and spoon over the mushrooms and sauce. Slice the steaks in half diagonally and place on top with any cooking juices. Sprinkle with pepper and a scant pinch of truffle salt, if using. Garnish with the remaining chives and serve immediately with griddled courgettes (see below).

For griddled courgettes, to serve as an accompaniment, thinly slice 2 courgettes lengthways. Heat a ridged griddle pan until very hot, add the courgettes and cook for 2–3 minutes on each side or until softened and charred.

herby chicken & ricotta cannelloni

Serves **4**
Preparation time **20 minutes**
Cooking time **40–50 minutes**

2 tablespoons **olive oil**
500 g (1 lb) boneless, skinless
    chicken thighs, finely
    chopped or minced
2 **leeks**, trimmed, cleaned and
    diced
500 ml (17 fl oz) **passata**
6 tablespoons chopped mixed
    herbs, such as **parsley,**
    chives, **sage**, **marjoram**
    and **dill**
1 teaspoon **fennel seeds**
250 g (8 oz) **ricotta cheese**
finely grated rind of 1 **lemon**
½ teaspoon **ground nutmeg**
1 teaspoon **sweet paprika**
100 g (3½ oz) **frozen**
    chopped spinach, thawed
75 g (3 oz) **sun-dried**
    tomatoes (not in oil),
    chopped (optional)
250 g (8 oz) **cannelloni tubes**
2–3 tablespoons finely grated
    Parmesan cheese
salt and **pepper**

Heat 1 tablespoon of the oil in a large, nonstick frying pan over a medium-high heat, add the chicken and fry for 3–4 minutes or until browned, stirring frequently. Reduce the heat slightly, add the leeks and cook for a further 3–4 minutes or until the leeks are translucent.

Meanwhile, heat the passata in a saucepan and stir in one-third of the chopped herbs, the fennel seeds and the remaining oil. Season with salt and pepper to taste, then simmer gently for 2–3 minutes.

Remove the chicken from the heat and stir in the ricotta, the remaining chopped herbs, the lemon rind, nutmeg, paprika, spinach and sun-dried tomatoes, if using. Season to taste. Stand the cannelloni tubes upright and use a narrow spoon to fill them with the ricotta mixture.

Spoon half of the passata over the base of a large, shallow ovenproof dish. Arrange the filled pasta tubes, side by side over the tomato sauce, so that they all fit in one closely fitting layer. Pour the remaining passata over the top of the cannelloni, then sprinkle with the Parmesan.

Place in a preheated oven, 180°C (350°F), Gas Mark 4, for 35–40 minutes or until cooked through and bubbling. Serve hot with a crisp green salad.

For chicken & ricotta lasagne, replace the chicken thighs with 250 g (8 oz) chopped cooked chicken and omit the leeks. Stir the chicken and fennel seeds into the ricotta mixture as above. Layer lasagne sheets with the chicken mixture and the passata. Sprinkle with Parmesan and cook as above.

chicken & barley risotto

Serves **4**
Preparation time **15 minutes**
Cooking time **about 1 hour 10 minutes**

2 tablespoons **olive oil**
6 boneless, skinless **chicken thighs**, diced
1 **onion**, roughly chopped
2 **garlic cloves**, finely chopped
200 g (7 oz) **chestnut mushrooms**, sliced
250 g (8 oz) **pearl barley**
200 ml (7 fl oz) **red wine**
1.2 litres (2 pints) **chicken stock**
salt and **pepper**
parsley leaves, to garnish
Parmesan cheese shavings, to serve

Heat the oil in a large frying pan over a medium-high heat, add the chicken and onion and fry for 5 minutes, stirring until lightly browned.

Stir in the garlic and mushrooms and fry for 2 minutes, then mix in the pearl barley. Add the red wine, half the stock and season with plenty of salt and pepper, then bring to the boil, stirring continuously. Reduce the heat, cover and simmer for 1 hour, topping up with extra stock as needed, until the chicken is cooked through and the barley is soft.

Spoon into shallow bowls and garnish with the parsley and sprinkle with Parmesan. Serve with garlic bread and salad, if liked.

For chicken & red rice risotto, fry the chicken and 1 chopped red onion as above. Add the garlic and 200 g (7 oz) skinned and diced tomatoes, omitting the mushrooms and pearl barley. Stir in 250 g (8 oz) red Camargue rice, cook for 1 minute, then add the red wine. Gradually add the hot stock a small ladleful at a time and stirring constantly, only adding more once the rice has absorbed the previous ladleful. Continue until all the liquid has been absorbed and the chicken and rice are tender. This should take about 25 minutes. Crumble 125 g (4 oz) St Agur or Roquefort cheese on top.

chicken & aduki bean salad

Serves **4**
Preparation time **15 minutes**
Cooking time **2–3 minutes**

1 **green pepper**, cored,
   deseeded and chopped
1 **red pepper**, cored,
   deseeded and chopped
1 small **red onion**, finely
   chopped
400 g (13 oz) can **aduki
   beans**, drained
200 g (7 oz) can **sweetcorn**,
   drained
1 small bunch of **coriander**,
   chopped
50 g (2 oz) unsweetened
   coconut chips or **flakes**
250 g (8 oz) cooked **chicken
   breast**, shredded
small handful of **alfalfa shoots**
   (optional)

Dressing
3 tablespoons **light
   groundnut oil**
2 tablespoons **light soy sauce**
2 teaspoons peeled and
   grated **fresh root ginger**
1 tablespoon **rice vinegar**

Mix together the green and red peppers, onion, aduki beans, sweetcorn and half the coriander in a large bowl. Whisk together the dressing ingredients in a separate bowl, then stir 3 tablespoons into the bean salad. Spoon the salad into serving dishes.

Place the coconut chips or flakes in a nonstick frying pan over a medium heat and dry-fry for 2–3 minutes or until lightly golden brown, stirring continuously.

Scatter the shredded chicken and remaining coriander leaves over the bean salad and sprinkle with the toasted coconut and alfalfa shoots, if using. Serve with the remaining dressing.

For prawn, avocado & coconut salad, make as above, replacing the chicken with 250 g (8 oz) cooked, peeled prawns. Dice the flesh of 1 firm, ripe avocado, toss in 1 tablespoon of lime juice and add to the bean salad. Serve as above.

thai red chicken curry

Serves **4**
Preparation time **15 minutes**
Cooking time **35 minutes**

1 tablespoon **sunflower oil**
3 **shallots**, finely chopped
3 **garlic cloves**, finely chopped
2 tablespoons **Thai red curry paste**
2 teaspoons **galangal paste**
400 ml (14 fl oz) can **reduced-fat coconut milk**
2 teaspoons **Thai fish sauce**
1 teaspoon **palm sugar** or **soft light brown sugar**
3 **kaffir lime leaves**
6 boneless, skinless **chicken thighs**, diced
handful of **Thai basil leaves** (optional)

Heat the oil in a saucepan over a medium heat, add the shallots and garlic and fry for 3–4 minutes until softened. Stir in the curry paste and galangal paste and cook for 1 minute. Mix in the coconut milk, fish sauce, sugar and lime leaves and bring to the boil.

Stir in the chicken, then reduce the heat, cover and simmer for 30 minutes, or until the chicken is cooked through, stirring occasionally. Stir in the basil leaves, if using, and serve with boiled rice.

For Thai green chicken curry, make the curry as above, adding 2 peeled and finely chopped lemon grass stalks when frying the shallots and garlic. Replace the red curry paste with 2 tablespoons Thai green curry paste and stir in, then continue as above. To finish, stir in the grated rind of 1 lime and lime juice to taste, garnish with chopped coriander and serve immediately.

lemony poached chicken

Serves **4**
Preparation time **10 minutes**
Cooking time **1¾–2 hours**

1 whole **free-range chicken**,
  about 1.5–2 kg (3–4 lb)
3 **shallots**, halved
2 **garlic cloves**, lightly crushed
1 **celery stick**, roughly
  chopped
1 **rosemary sprig**
8 **black peppercorns**
100 ml (3½ fl oz) **balsamic
  vinegar**
1 **preserved lemon**, chopped
1 small bunch of **sage**, leaves
  removed
2 tablespoons **extra virgin
  rapeseed oil**
salt and **pepper**

Place the chicken, shallots, garlic, celery, rosemary and black peppercorns in a large saucepan. Add the balsamic vinegar and pour in enough cold water to almost cover the chicken. Place over a medium heat and bring slowly to the boil, skimming the surface to remove any scummy froth. Cover and simmer gently for 1 hour.

Add the preserved lemon and half the sage leaves, then simmer gently for a further 15–30 minutes, depending on the size of the chicken, until the juices run clear when the thickest part of the leg is pierced with a knife. Carefully remove from the pan and place in a deep dish, cover with foil and leave to rest. Increase the heat and boil the stock for 20–25 minutes or until reduced by half. Remove from the heat and leave to cool slightly. Season to taste.

Heat the oil in a small frying pan and shallow-fry the remaining sage leaves for 30 seconds until crisp. Remove with a slotted spoon and drain on kitchen paper.

Cut the chicken meat from the carcass, discarding the skin, and spoon into shallow bowls with plenty of cooking broth. Garnish with the crisp sage leaves and serve with steamed asparagus and broccoli.

For lemony chicken breasts, replace the whole chicken with 4 large boneless, skinless chicken breasts. Place in a large saucepan with the garlic, rosemary, peppercorns, balsamic vinegar and preserved lemon and just cover with water. Simmer gently for about 12 minutes or until the chicken is cooked through. Cut the chicken into thick slices and serve in bowls with the chicken broth, garnished with sage leaves as above.

chicken & pickled walnut pilaf

Serves **4**
Preparation time **20 minutes**
Cooking time **about
35 minutes**

400 g (13 oz) boneless,
 skinless **chicken thighs**,
 diced
2 teaspoons **Moroccan
 spice blend** (see below for
 homemade)
4 tablespoons **olive oil**
50 g (2 oz) **pine nuts**
1 large **onion**, chopped
3 **garlic cloves**, sliced
½ teaspoon **ground turmeric**
250 g (8 oz) **mixed long-
 grain and wild rice**
300 ml (½ pint) **chicken stock**
3 pieces of **stem ginger**, finely
 chopped
3 tablespoons chopped
 parsley
2 tablespoons chopped **mint**
50 g (2 oz) **pickled walnuts**,
 sliced
salt and **pepper**

Mix the chicken with the spice blend and a little salt in
a bowl.

Heat the oil in a large frying pan over a medium heat,
add the pine nuts and fry until beginning to colour.
Remove with a slotted spoon and drain on kitchen
paper. Add the chicken to the pan and fry gently
for 6–8 minutes, or until lightly browned, stirring
occasionally.

Stir in the onion and fry for 5 minutes. Add the garlic
and turmeric and fry for a further 1 minute. Add the rice
and stock and bring to the boil, then reduce the heat
to low and simmer very gently for about 15 minutes or
until the chicken is cooked through, the rice is tender
and the stock absorbed. Add a little water if the liquid
has been absorbed before the rice is cooked through.

Stir in the ginger, parsley, mint, walnuts and pine nuts.
Season with salt and pepper to taste and heat through
gently for 2 minutes before serving.

For homemade Moroccan spice blend, mix together
½ teaspoon each of crushed fennel, cumin, coriander
and mustard seeds with ¼ teaspoon each of ground
cloves and cinnamon.

asian minced turkey salad

Serves **4**
Preparation time **20 minutes**
Cooking time **8–10 minutes**

500 g (1 lb) **minced turkey**
2 **garlic cloves**, finely chopped
1 **shallot**, finely chopped
1 small **red chilli**, deseeded
    and finely chopped
1 ½ tablespoons **groundnut oil**
½ **Chinese cabbage**,
    shredded
150 g (5 oz) **mangetout**,
    shredded
½ small **cucumber**, cut into
    thin matchsticks
250 g (8 oz) **bean sprouts**
1 **carrot**, peeled and cut into
    thin matchsticks
3 **spring onions**, thinly sliced
4 tablespoons **unsalted**
    peanuts, chopped
chopped **coriander**

Dressing
1 ½ teaspoons peeled and
    grated **fresh root ginger**
1 ½ teaspoons **fish sauce**
1 tablespoon **light soy sauce**
2 tablespoons **lime juice**
2 tablespoons **groundnut oil**
1 ½ teaspoons **palm sugar**

Mix together the turkey, garlic, shallot and chilli in a bowl. Heat the oil in a large frying pan over a medium-high heat, add the turkey mixture and then stir-fry for 8–10 minutes or until the meat is browned and cooked through. Tip into a large bowl.

Whisk together all the dressing ingredients in a small bowl and pour over the cooked turkey. Leave to cool for 10 minutes.

Meanwhile, mix together the Chinese cabbage, mangetout, cucumber, bean sprouts, carrot and spring onions in a bowl. Pile on to serving plates and spoon over the turkey. Sprinkle with the peanuts and coriander and serve immediately with lime wedges on the side.

For Asian-style pork parcels, replace the turkey with 500 g (1 lb) minced pork. Prepare as above, keeping the Chinese cabbage whole and separate from the salad. Serve the whole leaves, dressed pork and salad in 3 separate piles. To eat, pile the mixed salad and minced pork into the whole leaves, sprinkle with the coriander and peanuts and fold to create a parcel before eating.

duck, pear & pomegranate salad

Serves **4**
Preparation time **15 minutes**
Cooking time **15–20 minutes**

2 large, lean **duck breasts**
2 **Comice pears**, cored and diced
125 g (4 oz) **mixed leaf and herb salad**
50 g (2 oz) **walnut pieces**
1 **pomegranate**, seeds removed

Dressing
2 teaspoons **lime juice**
2 teaspoons **raspberry vinegar**
2 teaspoons **pomegranate molasses** (optional – see right for homemade)
2 tablespoons **walnut oil**
salt and **pepper**

Remove any excess fat from the duck breasts and score the surface using a sharp knife. Heat a ridged griddle pan until hot, then add the duck breasts, skin side down, and cook for 8–10 minutes. Turn them over and cook for a further 5–10 minutes or until cooked to the pinkness desired. Remove from the pan, cover with foil and leave to rest.

Mix together the pears and leaf salad in a bowl. Arrange on serving plates and scatter with the walnut pieces.

Whisk together all the dressing ingredients in a bowl and season to taste. Drizzle over the salad.

Slice the duck breasts and arrange on the salad. Scatter over the pomegranate seeds and serve immediately.

For homemade pomegranate molasses, juice 2 large pomegranates with a citrus press or remove the seeds and pulse in a food processor or blender. Pour the juice into a small saucepan, add 1 tablespoon sugar and stir until the sugar dissolves. Bring to the boil, then reduce the heat and simmer rapidly until reduced to a thick, sticky molasses. Cool and store in an airtight bottle in the refrigerator for up to 2 weeks.

vegetarian

lemony mushroom spaghetti

Serves **4**
Preparation time **8 minutes**
Cooking time **18–20 minutes**

250 g (8 oz) **chestnut mushrooms**
1 **garlic clove**, finely chopped
2 tablespoons **olive oil**
400 g (13 oz) **wholewheat spaghetti**
150 g (5 oz) fresh **wholemeal breadcrumbs**
finely grated rind and juice of
  1 **lemon**
1 small bunch of **parsley**, chopped
½ teaspoon **chilli flakes** (optional)
salt and **pepper**
grated **Parmesan cheese**, to serve (optional)

Place the mushrooms, stalk side up, in a large roasting tin. Scatter with the garlic, drizzle with the oil and season generously with salt and pepper. Place in a preheated oven, 180°C (350°F), Gas Mark 4, for 18–20 minutes or until tender and juicy.

Meanwhile, cook the pasta in a large saucepan of boiling water for 10–12 minutes, or according to the packet instructions, until al dente.

Put the breadcrumbs, lemon rind, half of the parsley and the chilli flakes, if using, into a large, nonstick frying pan over a medium high heat. Dry-fry for 4–5 minutes, or until golden brown and crispy, stirring continuously. Set aside.

Remove the mushrooms from the oven and cool slightly, then roughly chop. Drain the pasta and toss with the mushrooms, lemon juice and remaining parsley. Season with salt and pepper to taste, then heap into serving bowls. Scatter over the breadcrumbs and serve immediately with Parmesan, if liked.

For wild mushroom pasta, cook the spaghetti as above. Roughly chop 150 g (5 oz) chestnut mushrooms. Heat the oil in a large frying pan over a medium-high heat, then add the mushrooms and garlic and fry for 3–4 minutes until softened. Roughly chop a drained 280 g (9 oz) jar mixed or wild mushrooms, add to the pan and heat through. Stir in the lemon juice and rind, chopped parsley and chilli flakes, if using. Toss with the drained pasta, season to taste and serve.

penne with peas & beans

Serves **4**
Preparation time **5 minutes**
Cooking time **10–12 minutes**

400 g (13 oz) **wholewheat penne**
1 tablespoon **extra virgin rapeseed oil** or **olive oil**
2 **spring onions**, finely chopped
250 g (8 oz) **reduced-fat mascarpone cheese**
4 tablespoons **lemon juice**
250 g (8 oz) **frozen peas**, thawed
250 g (8 oz) **frozen baby broad beans**, thawed
1 small bunch of **basil**, roughly chopped, a few leaves reserved for garnish
salt and **pepper**

Cook the penne in a large saucepan of boiling water for 10–12 minutes, or according to the packet instructions, until al dente.

Meanwhile, heat the oil in a large frying pan over a medium-low heat, add the spring onions and fry for 1–2 minutes or until softened. Stir in the mascarpone, lemon juice, peas, broad beans and basil. Season with salt and pepper to taste and stir for 1–2 minutes or until bubbling.

Drain the penne, reserving 3 tablespoons of the cooking water. Stir the pasta and the reserved liquid into the creamy peas and beans. Serve immediately, garnished with extra basil leaves.

For broad bean & pea risotto, melt 25 g (1 oz) butter with 1 tablespoon olive oil and cook the spring onions until softened. Add 350 g (11½ oz) risotto rice and stir for 1–2 minutes or until translucent. Add 200 ml (7 fl oz) white wine, then 1 litre (1¾ pints) boiling vegetable stock, a small ladleful at a time and stirring constantly only adding more once the rice has absorbed the previous ladleful. Continue until all the liquid has been absorbed and the rice is just cooked. This should take about 18 minutes. Stir in the peas, beans and basil 2 minutes before the end of the cooking time. Remove from the heat, stir in 125 g (4 oz) mascarpone and serve immediately.

spicy lentils & chickpeas

Serves **4**
Preparation time **15 minutes**
Cooking time **about
35 minutes**

1 tablespoon **groundnut oil**
1 **onion**, finely chopped
2 **garlic cloves**, thinly sliced
2 **celery sticks**, diced
1 **green pepper**, cored,
    deseeded and chopped
150 g (5 oz) **red lentils**, rinsed
2 teaspoons **garam masala**
1 teaspoon **cumin seeds**
½ teaspoon **hot chilli powder**
1 teaspoon **ground coriander**
2 tablespoons **tomato purée**
750 ml (1¼ pints) hot
    vegetable stock
400 g (13 oz) can **chickpeas**,
    drained
salt and **pepper**
2 tablespoons chopped
    coriander, to garnish

Heat the oil in a heavy-based saucepan over a medium heat, add the onion, garlic, celery and green pepper and fry gently for 10–12 minutes or until softened and beginning to colour.

Stir in the lentils and spices and cook for 2–3 minutes, stirring frequently. Add the tomato purée, stock and chickpeas and bring to the boil. Reduce the heat, cover and simmer gently for about 20 minutes or until the lentils collapse. Season with salt and pepper to taste.

Ladle into bowls and sprinkle with the coriander. Serve immediately with boiled brown rice and cooling, spiced yogurt (see below).

For cooling, spiced yogurt, to serve as an accompaniment, mix together 200 g (7 oz) fat-free natural yogurt, 2 tablespoons lemon juice and ½ teaspoon of garam masala in a small bowl. Fold in ½ small, deseeded and grated cucumber, then season with salt and pepper to taste. Serve sprinkled with 1 tablespoon chopped coriander.

veggie stir-fry with pak choi

Serves **4**
Preparation time **10 minutes**
Cooking time **5–7 minutes**

8 small **pak choi**, about 625 g
  (1¼ lb) in total
1 tablespoon **groundnut oil**
2 **garlic cloves**, thinly sliced
2.5 cm (1 inch) piece of **fresh
  root ginger**, peeled and
  finely chopped
200 g (7 oz) **sugar snap
  peas**, sliced diagonally
200 g (7 oz) **asparagus tips**,
  sliced in half lengthways
200 g (7 oz) **baby corn**, sliced
  in half lengthways
120 g (4 oz) podded
  edamame beans or 200 g
  (7 oz) **bean sprouts**
150 ml (¼ pint) **sweet teriyaki
  sauce**

Cut the pak choi in half, or into thick slices if large, and put in a steamer basket. Lower into a shallow saucepan of boiling water so that the pak choi is not quite touching the water. Cover and steam for 2–3 minutes or until tender. Alternatively, use a bamboo or electric steamer.

Heat a large wok or frying pan over a high heat until smoking hot, add the oil, garlic and ginger and stir-fry for 30 seconds. Add the vegetables and stir continuously for 2–3 minutes or until beginning to wilt.

Pour over the sweet teriyaki sauce, toss to combine and serve immediately with the steamed pak choi and steamed rice, if liked.

For sweet chilli vegetable stir-fry, heat the oil in the wok and stir-fry 1 thinly sliced onion with the garlic and ginger. Add 1 carrot, cut into thin matchsticks, and 200 g (7 oz) sliced mushrooms and stir-fry for 2 minutes. Stir in 200 g (7 oz) bean sprouts and 300 g (10 oz) shredded spinach for a further minute until wilted. Stir in 200 ml (7 fl oz) sweet chilli stir-fry sauce and serve immediately with the pak choi or cooked noodles.

roasted peppers with quinoa

Serves **4**
Preparation time **15 minutes**
Cooking time **45 minutes**

2 romano or **long red
    peppers**, halved, cored and
    deseeded
2 large **yellow peppers**,
    halved, cored and deseeded
20 **red** and **yellow cherry
    tomatoes**, halved
1 teaspoon **cumin seeds**
2 tablespoons **olive oil**
200 g (7 oz) **quinoa**
1 **onion**, finely chopped
½ teaspoon **ground ginger**
1 teaspoon **paprika**
pinch of **nutmeg**
50 g (2 oz) ready-to-eat **dried
    apricots**, chopped
50 g (2 oz) **raisins**
50 g (2 oz) stoned **dates**,
    chopped
50 g (2 oz) shelled **pistachio
    nuts**
25 g (1 oz) **flaked almonds**,
    toasted, plus extra to garnish
2 **spring onions**, finely sliced
salt and **pepper**

Fill the red peppers with the yellow cherry tomatoes and the yellow peppers with the red tomatoes. Scatter over the cumin seeds, drizzle with 1 tablespoon of the oil and season well with salt and pepper. Place in a preheated oven, 180°C (350°F), Gas Mark 4, for about 45 minutes or until tender and slightly blackened around the edges.

Meanwhile, rinse the quinoa several times in cold water. Pour into a pan with twice its volume of boiling water, cover and simmer for about 12 minutes. It is cooked when the seed is coming away from the germ. Remove from the heat, cover and leave to stand until all the water has been absorbed.

Heat the remaining oil in a small frying pan over a medium heat, add the onion and cook for 10 minutes or until softened. Add the spices, dried fruits and nuts and cook for a further 3–4 minutes, or until the fruits have softened, stirring frequently. Gently fold into the cooked quinoa.

Heap the quinoa on to 4 plates and top each with 1 red and 1 yellow pepper half. Sprinkle with the spring onions and extra flaked almonds and serve.

For quinoa-stuffed peppers, make the fruit and nut quinoa as above. Cut 10 cherry tomatoes into quarters and mix with the quinoa. Spoon into the halved peppers and top with 150 g (5 oz) sliced reduced-fat feta or goats' cheese. Drizzle with a little olive oil, the cumin seeds and season with salt and pepper. Place in the oven for 45 minutes or until the peppers are tender. Serve as above with salad leaves.

veggie kebabs with bulgar wheat

Serves **4**
Preparation time **20 minutes**
Cooking time **20–25 minutes**

1 small **red pepper**, cored and
    deseeded
1 small **yellow pepper**, cored
    and deseeded
2 small **courgettes**, thickly
    sliced
1 small **aubergine**, cut into
    chunks
1 small **red onion**, quartered
8 **chestnut mushrooms**,
    halved
2 teaspoons **dried rosemary**
2 tablespoons **olive oil**
grated rind of 1 **lemon**
1 teaspoon **fennel seeds**
salt and **pepper**

Bulgar wheat salad
700 ml (23 fl oz) **vegetable
    stock**
250 g (8 oz) **coarse bulgar
    wheat**
1 tablespoon **harissa**
75 g (3 oz) **raisins**
2 **spring onions**, finely sliced
2 tablespoons chopped **mint**
50 g (2 oz) **sunflower seeds**

Cut the red and yellow peppers into large pieces and
place in a bowl with the other vegetables. Toss with
the dried rosemary, oil, lemon rind and fennel seeds
and season with salt and pepper. Thread on to 4 long
or 8 short metal skewers and cook under a medium-hot
grill for 20–25 minutes, or until tender and browned,
turning occasionally.

Meanwhile, put the stock in a saucepan and bring to
the boil. Add the bulgar wheat, cover and simmer for
7 minutes. Remove from the heat and leave to stand
until the liquid has been absorbed. Fork the harissa,
raisins, spring onions, mint and sunflower seeds through
the cooked bulgar wheat until well combined, then
spoon on to serving plates.

Arrange the vegetable kebabs on the plates with the
bulgar wheat salad and serve immediately.

For minted yogurt, to serve as an accompaniment,
mix together 250 g (8 oz) fat-free Greek yogurt,
½ teaspoon fennel seeds, 2 tablespoons lemon juice
and 3 tablespoons chopped mint in a serving dish and
season to taste.

squash, carrot & mango tagine

Serves **4**
Preparation time **15 minutes**
Cooking time **35–40 minutes**

2 tablespoons **olive oil**
1 large **onion**, cut into large
   chunks
3 **garlic cloves**, finely chopped
1 **butternut squash**, about
   875 g (1¾ lb) in total,
   peeled, deseeded and cubed
2 small **carrots**, peeled and
   cut into thick batons
½ x 2.5 cm (1 inch) **cinnamon
   stick**
½ teaspoon **turmeric**
¼ teaspoon **cayenne pepper**
   (optional)
½ teaspoon ground **cumin**
1 teaspoon **paprika**
pinch of **saffron threads**
1 tablespoon **tomato purée**
750 ml (1¼ pints) hot
   vegetable stock
1 **mango**, peeled, stoned
   and cut into 2.5 cm (1 inch)
   chunks
salt and **pepper**
2 tablespoons chopped
   coriander, to garnish

Heat the oil in a large, heavy-based saucepan over a
medium heat, add the onion and cook for 5 minutes or
until beginning to soften. Add the garlic, squash, carrots
and spices and fry gently for a further 5 minutes.

Stir in the tomato purée, then pour in the stock and
season with salt and pepper to taste. Cover and simmer
gently for 20–25 minutes or until the vegetables are
tender. Stir in the mango and simmer gently for a
further 5 minutes.

Ladle the tagine into serving bowls and sprinkle with
the coriander and serve with steamed couscous.

For spicy squash & carrot soup, make the tagine
as above, adding an extra 250 ml (8 fl oz) vegetable
stock. Once the vegetables are tender, place in a food
processor or blender and blend until smooth. Ladle into
bowls and serve scattered with the chopped coriander.

roasted beetroot & bean salad

Serves **4**
Preparation time **10 minutes**
Cooking time **about 1 hour
10 minutes**

1 kg (2 lb) raw **beetroot**,
    peeled
1½ tablespoons **extra virgin
    rapeseed oil**, plus extra to
    serve
2 teaspoons **cumin seeds**
4 tablespoons **balsamic
    vinegar**
250 g (8 oz) **green beans**,
    trimmed
1 **red onion**, thinly sliced
250 g (8 oz) **ricotta cheese**
finely grated rind of 1 **lemon**
1 small bunch of **basil**,
    chopped, a few leaves
    reserved for garnish
1 **multi-grain** or **cereal
    baguette**, sliced
1 tablespoon **balsamic glaze**
salt and **pepper**

Cut the beetroot into wedges or in half, if small. Toss with the oil and cumin seeds and season with salt and pepper. Tip into a roasting tin and place in a preheated oven, 180°C (350°F), Gas Mark 4, for 45 minutes. Pour over the balsamic vinegar and toss to coat. Return to the oven for a further 20 minutes or until the beetroot is tender and slightly sticky.

Cook the beans in a large saucepan of lightly salted boiling water for 2–3 minutes or until just tender. Drain and toss with the beetroot and onion in a bowl.

Mix together in a bowl the ricotta, lemon rind and basil and season with salt and pepper. Spread over the baguette slices, place on a grill pan and cook under a preheated medium-hot grill for 3 minutes or until hot and lightly golden.

Heap the beetroot and bean salad into bowls and top with the ricotta croutons. Drizzle with a little balsamic glaze and extra virgin rapeseed oil and scatter with the extra basil leaves. Serve immediately.

For wintery roast parsnip & carrot salad, mix together 500 g (1 lb) parsnips and 500 g (1 lb) carrots, both cut into batons, the oil, cumin seeds and 3–4 thyme sprigs in a roasting tin. Place in the preheated oven for about 30 minutes or until tender. Spoon into a serving dish and drizzle over 2 tablespoons runny honey mixed with 1 tablespoon balsamic vinegar. Make the croutons as above, replacing the basil with 1 bunch of thyme. Serve the roast vegetables with salad leaves, scattered with 2 tablespoons toasted hazelnuts, if liked.

chickpea & feta salad

Serves **4**
Preparation time **10 minutes**
Cooking time **5–7 minutes**

400 g (13 oz) can **chickpeas**,
   drained
1 **Lebanese cucumber** or
   ½ **cucumber**, diced
150 g (5 oz) **radishes**, thinly
   sliced
150 g (5 oz) **red seedless
   grapes**, halved
1 small **radicchio**, sliced
200 g (7 oz) **reduced-fat feta
   cheese**, cut into 4 pieces
2 tablespoons **extra virgin
   rapeseed** or **olive oil**
½ teaspoon **dried oregano**
2 heaped tablespoons
   pumpkin seeds
small handful of **radish
   sprouts** (optional)
salt and **pepper**
lemon wedges, to serve

Mix together the chickpeas, cucumber, radishes and grapes in a large bowl. Toss lightly with the radicchio, season with salt and pepper and pile into serving dishes.

Place the feta on a foil-lined grill pan, drizzle with 2 teaspoons of the oil and sprinkle with the dried oregano and a little pepper. Cook under a preheated grill for 3–4 minutes or until golden. Remove from the grill and leave to cool for 2–3 minutes.

Heat a small nonstick frying pan over a medium heat, add the pumpkin seeds and dry-fry for 2–3 minutes or until lightly golden. Tip on to a small plate.

Arrange the grilled feta on the salad. Scatter over the toasted pumpkin seeds and radish sprouts, if using. Drizzle with the remaining oil and serve immediately with the lemon wedges.

For watermelon & haloumi salad, mix together ½ peeled watermelon, cut into large chunks, with 2 tablespoons chopped mint, ½ finely chopped red onion, 16–20 pitted black olives and the chickpeas. Replace the feta with 200 g (7 oz) haloumi cheese and cut into slices. Brush with the oil and grill as above. Serve with the pumpkin seeds as above.

baked mushroom risotto

Serves **4**
Preparation time **15 minutes**
Cooking time 1¼ **hours**

30 g (1½ oz) **dried porcini**
   mushrooms, soaked in
   125 ml (4 fl oz) boiling water
   for 10–15 minutes
25 g (1 oz) **butter**
1 tablespoon **olive oil**
2 **shallots**, finely chopped
1 **leek**, trimmed, cleaned and
   finely chopped
1 large **garlic clove**, finely
   chopped
350 g (11½ oz) **short-grain**
   brown rice
50 ml (2 fl oz) **Marsala**
1.2 litres (2 pints) **vegetable**
   stock
125 g (4 oz) **asparagus tips**,
   chopped
salt and **pepper**
finely grated **Parmesan**
   cheese, to serve (optional)

Drain the porcini, reserving the soaking liquid, then squeeze dry and roughly chop.

Heat the butter and oil in a large, flameproof casserole over a low heat, add the shallots and leek and fry gently for 8 minutes or until softened. Add the garlic and fry for a further 2 minutes. Stir the rice into the pan and cook for 1–2 minutes, then pour over the Marsala and bubble, stirring continuously, until evaporated.

Mix in the mushrooms, reserved soaking liquid and stock, stir well and bring to the boil. Season to taste with salt and pepper, cover and place in a preheated oven, 180°C (350°F), Gas Mark 4, for 45 minutes, stirring occasionally.

Add the asparagus and stir well. Return to the oven for a further 15 minutes or until the rice is tender and most of the liquid has been absorbed. Remove from the oven and leave to stand for 2–3 minutes. Spoon the risotto into serving bowls and sprinkle with the grated Parmesan, if liked.

For Asian-style baked risotto, make as above, replacing the porcini mushrooms with 30 g (1½ oz) dried shiitake mushrooms, the Marsala with 50 ml (2 fl oz) sake, the vegetable stock with 1.2 litres (2 pints) instant miso soup and the asparagus tips with 2 small, sliced pak choi.

artichoke & asparagus pizzas

Serves **4**

Preparation time **20 minutes**, plus proving

Cooking time **45 minutes**

400 g (13 oz) **wholemeal flour**

1 x 5 g (¼ oz) **sachet fast-action dried yeast**

2 teaspoons **sugar,** plus a pinch

1½ teaspoons **salt**

2 tablespoons **olive oil**

225 ml (7½ fl oz) hand-hot **water**

2 **garlic cloves,** finely chopped

300 g (10 oz) **basil** and **onion passata**

1½ teaspoons **dried oregano**

400 g (13 oz) can **artichokes** in water, drained and thickly sliced

200 g (7 oz) **asparagus tips**

250 g (8 oz) **ricotta cheese**

100 g (3½ oz) finely grated **reduced-fat extra mature Cheddar cheese** (optional)

handful of **rocket leaves**

chilli oil, for drizzling (optional)

salt and **pepper**

Put the flour, yeast, 2 teaspoons sugar and the salt in a bowl. Pour in 1 tablespoon of the oil and measurement water and mix to a dough. Turn the dough out onto a lightly floured surface and knead for 4–5 minutes until smooth and elastic. Place in a lightly oiled bowl, cover with oiled clingfilm and leave in a warm place to rise for 1½ hours or until doubled in size.

Meanwhile, heat the remaining oil in a saucepan over a low heat, add the garlic and cook for 1 minute. Stir in the passata, ½ teaspoon of the oregano and a pinch of sugar and season with salt and pepper to taste. Simmer for 30 minutes or until thick. Heat a griddle pan, add the artichokes and cook for 3–4 minutes, turning once, or until slightly charred. Repeat with the asparagus.

Divide the dough into 4 and roll out on a floured surface until about 20 cm (8 inches) in diameter. Place the bases on lightly greased baking sheets, cover and leave to rise for a further 30–45 minutes. Thinly spread the sauce over the bases and arrange the griddled vegetables on top. Add teaspoons of ricotta and the Cheddar, if using. Scatter over the remaining oregano.

Place in a preheated oven, 200°C (400°F), Gas Mark 6, for 12–15 minutes or until bubbling and the bases are crisp. Serve topped with the rocket and drizzled with a little chilli oil, if liked.

For quick pitta pizzas, spread a little basil and garlic passata over 4 wholemeal pitta breads. Top with 200 g (7 oz) char-grilled vegetables and the ricotta, Cheddar and oregano, as above. Place under a preheated grill for 4–5 minutes or until golden and bubbling.

warm lentil, tomato & onion salad

Serves **4**
Preparation time **10 minutes**
Cooking time **40–45 minutes**

1 tablespoon **olive oil**
1 large **red onion**, thinly sliced
50 g (2 oz) **fresh root ginger**,
   peeled and chopped
4 **garlic cloves**, thinly sliced
125 g (4 oz) **green lentils**,
   rinsed
100 g (3½ oz) **red lentils**,
   rinsed
½ teaspoon **ground
   cinnamon**
400 g (13 oz) **tomatoes**,
   roughly chopped, or
   400 g (13 oz) can **chopped
   tomatoes**
350 ml (12 fl oz) **water** or
   vegetable stock
2 teaspoons **black onion
   seeds**
salt and **pepper**
parsley, to garnish
lemon wedges, to serve

Heat the oil in a large, heavy-based saucepan over
a medium-low heat, add the onion, ginger and garlic
and cook gently for 10 minutes until softened but not
coloured.

Stir the lentils and cinnamon into the onions. Add
the tomatoes and measurement water or stock.
Season with salt and pepper and bring to the boil.
Reduce the heat, cover and leave to simmer gently for
30–35 minutes or until the lentils are tender and the
liquid has been absorbed.

Spoon the lentils into bowls and sprinkle with the
black onion seeds and garnish with parsley leaves.
Serve warm with lemon wedges and toasted wholemeal
flatbreads, if liked.

For no-cook lentil, tomato & onion salad, rinse
and drain a 250 g (8 oz) pack cooked lentils. Place
in a bowl and mix with ½ finely chopped red onion,
4 chopped tomatoes, a small crushed garlic clove, a
1 cm (½ inch) piece of peeled and finely grated fresh
root ginger and 2 tablespoons chopped parsley. Make
a dressing with 1 tablespoon olive oil, 2 tablespoons
lemon juice, pinch of ground cinnamon, pinch of ground
paprika and some salt and pepper. Toss the lentil salad
in the dressing and serve, garnished, as above.

bean chilli with avocado salsa

Serves **4–6**
Preparation time **15 minutes**
Cooking time **30 minutes**

3 tablespoons **olive oil**
2 teaspoons **cumin seeds**,
  crushed
1 teaspoon **dried oregano**
1 **red onion**, chopped
1 **celery stick**, chopped
1 **red chilli**, deseeded and
  sliced
2 x 400 g (13 oz) cans
  chopped tomatoes
50 g (2 oz) **sun-dried
  tomatoes**, thinly sliced
2 teaspoons **sugar**
300 ml (½ pint) **vegetable
  stock**
2 x 400 g (13 oz) cans **red
  kidney beans**, drained
handful of **coriander,** chopped
100 g (3½ oz) **low-fat soured
  cream**
salt and **pepper**

Salsa
1 small **avocado**
2 **tomatoes**
2 tablespoons **sweet chilli
  sauce**
2 teaspoons **lime juice**

Heat the oil in a large saucepan over a medium-low heat, add the cumin seeds, oregano, onion, celery and chilli and cook gently, stirring frequently, for about 6–8 minutes or until the vegetables are beginning to colour.

Add the canned tomatoes, sun-dried tomatoes, sugar, stock, beans and coriander and bring to the boil. Reduce the heat and simmer for about 20 minutes or until the juices are thickened and pulpy.

Make the salsa. Peel, stone and finely dice the avocado and put it in a small bowl. Halve the tomatoes, scoop out the seeds and finely dice the flesh. Add to the bowl along with the chilli sauce and lime juice. Mix well.

Season the bean mixture with salt and pepper and spoon into bowls. Top with spoonfuls of soured cream and the avocado salsa. Serve with toasted pitta or flatbreads.

For bean stew, heat 4 tablespoons olive oil in a small saucepan, add 2 crushed garlic cloves, 1 tablespoon chopped rosemary and 2 teaspoons grated lemon rind and gently fry for 3 minutes. Add 2 x 400 g (13 oz) cans butter beans with their liquid, 4 large skinned and chopped tomatoes and a little chilli powder. Bring to the boil, then simmer over a high heat for 8–10 minutes or until the sauce is thickened. Season and serve with the avocado salsa and soured cream.

gingered tofu & mango salad

Serves **2**

Preparation time **15 minutes**, plus marinating

Cooking time **5 minutes**

25 g (1 oz) **fresh root ginger**, peeled and grated

2 tablespoons **light soy sauce**

1 **garlic clove**, finely chopped

1 tablespoon **seasoned rice vinegar**

125 g (4 oz) **firm silken tofu**, cut into 1 cm (½ inch) cubes

2 tablespoons **groundnut** or **vegetable oil**

1 bunch of **spring onions**, sliced diagonally into 1.5 cm (¾ inch) lengths

40 g (1½ oz) **cashew nuts**

1 small **mango**, peeled, stoned and sliced

½ small **iceberg lettuce**, shredded

Mix together the ginger, soy sauce, garlic and vinegar in a small bowl. Add the tofu to the bowl and toss the ingredients together. Leave to marinate for 15 minutes.

Lift the tofu from the marinade with a fork, drain it and reserve the marinade. Heat the oil in a frying pan over a medium heat, add the tofu pieces and gently fry for 3 minutes or until golden. Remove with a slotted spoon and keep warm.

Add the spring onions and cashews to the pan and fry quickly for 30 seconds. Add the mango slices to the pan and cook for 30 seconds or until heated through.

Pile the lettuce on to serving plates and scatter the tofu, spring onions, mango and cashews over the top. Heat the marinade juices in the pan with 2 tablespoons water, pour the mixture over the salad and serve immediately.

For tofu & sugar snap salad, marinate and fry the tofu as above. Add the spring onions and cashews to the pan, also adding 1 red chilli, sliced into rounds, and 100 g (3½ oz) halved sugar snap peas. Omit the mango. Fry for 1 minute until heated through, then gently toss in the fried tofu. Add the juice of ½ lime and 2 tablespoons water to the reserved marinade and drizzle it over the salad before serving on the lettuce.

pumpkin & root vegetable stew

Serves **8–10**
Preparation time **20 minutes**
Cooking time **1½–2 hours**

1 **pumpkin**, about 1.5 kg (3 lb)
4 tablespoons **sunflower** or
    olive oil
1 large **onion**, finely chopped
3–4 **garlic cloves**, finely
    chopped
1 small **red chilli**, deseeded
    and chopped
4 **celery sticks**, cut into
    2.5 cm (1 inch) lengths
500 g (1 lb) **carrots**, cut into
    2.5 cm (1 inch) pieces
250 g (8 oz) **parsnips**, cut into
    2.5 cm (1 inch) pieces
2 x 400g (13 oz) cans **plum**
    tomatoes
3 tablespoons **tomato purée**
1–2 tablespoons **hot paprika**
250 ml (8 fl oz) **vegetable**
    stock
1 **bouquet garni**
2 x 400 g (13 oz) cans **red**
    kidney beans, drained
salt and **pepper**
3–4 tablespoons finely
    chopped **parsley**, to garnish

Slice the pumpkin in half and discard the seeds and fibres. Cut the flesh into cubes, removing the skin. You should have about 1 kg (2 lb) pumpkin flesh.

Heat the oil in a large saucepan over a medium heat, add the onion, garlic and chilli and fry until softened but not coloured. Add the pumpkin and celery and fry gently for 10 minutes.

Stir in the carrots, parsnips, tomatoes, tomato purée, paprika, stock and bouquet garni. Bring to the boil, then reduce the heat, cover the pan and simmer for 1–1½ hours or until the vegetables are almost tender.

Add the beans and cook for 10 minutes. Season with salt and pepper and sprinkle with the parsley. Serve with crusty bread or garlic mashed potatoes. This stew improves with reheating.

For pumpkin goulash, heat 2 tablespoons oil in a large, heavy-based saucepan and fry 1 chopped onion until softened. Stir in 1 tablespoon paprika and 1 teaspoon caraway seeds and cook for 1 minute. Add a 400 g (13 oz) can chopped tomatoes and 2 tablespoons soft dark brown sugar and bring to the boil. Add 375 g (12 oz) thickly sliced pumpkin, 250 g (8 oz) diced potatoes, a large sliced carrot and 1 deseeded and chopped red pepper. Season, cover and bring to the boil, then simmer for 1–1½ hours. To serve, stir in 150 ml (¼ pint) low-fat soured cream.

saffron-scented vegetable tagine

Serves **4**
Preparation time **15 minutes**
Cooking time **50 minutes**

100 ml (3½ fl oz) **sunflower
  oil**
1 large **onion**, finely chopped
2 **garlic cloves**, finely chopped
2 teaspoons **ground
  coriander**
2 teaspoons **ground cumin**
2 teaspoons **ground
  cinnamon**
400 g (13 oz) can **chickpeas**,
  drained
400 g (13 oz) can **chopped
  tomatoes**
600 ml (1 pint) **vegetable
  stock**
¼ teaspoon **saffron threads**
1 large **aubergine**, chopped
250 g (8 oz) **button
  mushrooms**, halved if large
100 g (3½ oz) **dried figs**,
  chopped
2 tablespoons chopped
  coriander
salt and **pepper**

Heat 2 tablespoons of the oil in a frying pan over a
medium heat, add the onion, garlic and spices and cook,
stirring frequently, for 5 minutes or until golden. Using
a slotted spoon, transfer to a saucepan and add the
chickpeas, tomatoes, stock and saffron. Season with
salt and pepper.

Heat the remaining oil in the frying pan over a high
heat, add the aubergine and cook, stirring frequently, for
5 minutes or until browned. Add to the stew and bring
to the boil, then reduce the heat, cover and simmer
gently for 20 minutes.

Stir in the mushrooms and figs and simmer gently,
uncovered, for a further 20 minutes. Stir in the chopped
coriander and season to taste. Serve with steamed
wholewheat couscous.

For winter vegetable & lentil tagine, replace the
aubergine with 2 sliced carrots and 2 cubed potatoes.
Instead of the chickpeas use a drained 400 g (13 oz)
can green lentils. Make as above, replacing the figs with
100 g (3½ oz) ready-to-eat dried apricots.

and to finish...

elderflower poached pears

Serves **4**

Preparation time **5 minutes**, plus cooling

Cooking time **about 25 minutes**

125 ml (4 fl oz) **elderflower and pear** or **elderflower and apple cordial**

500 ml (17 fl oz) **apple juice**

2 teaspoons **lemon juice**

4 large **pears**, peeled, cored and quartered

pinch of **saffron threads**

Mix the cordial, apple juice and lemon juice in a small, deep saucepan. Bring to a gentle simmer and add the pears and saffron. Simmer gently for about 25 minutes or until the pears are tender.

Remove from the heat, cover and leave to cool completely in the poaching liquid. Carefully remove the pears with a slotted spoon and divide into serving bowls. Ladle over the poaching liquid to serve.

For baked apples in elderflower & saffron, replace the pears with 4 peeled, cored and quartered apples and place in a deep ovenproof dish. Heat the cordial, apple juice and saffron as above, omitting the lemon juice, and pour over the apples. Cover with foil and place in a preheated oven, 180°C (350 °C), Gas Mark 4, for about 1 hour or until the apples are tender.

autumn fruit oaty crumble

Serves **4**
Preparation time **15 minutes**
Cooking time **40–45 minutes**

1 **dessert apple**, peeled,
  cored and sliced
25 g (1 oz) ready-to-eat **dried
  apples**, chopped (optional)
400 g (13 oz) can **pear
  halves** in juice, drained with
  4 tablespoons juice reserved,
  roughly chopped
200 g (7 oz) ripe **plums**,
  halved, stoned and quartered
25 g (1 oz) **raisins** or **golden
  raisins**

Topping
75 g (3 oz) **wholemeal flour**
50 g (2 oz) **rolled oats**
25 g (1 oz) **bran**
pinch of **salt**
50 g (2 oz) **pecan nuts**,
  chopped
2 tablespoons **soft dark
  brown sugar**
¾ teaspoon **mixed spice**
75 g (3 oz) **butter**, melted

Put all of the prepared fruit and raisins into a shallow, rectangular ovenproof dish, approximately 28 x 20 cm (11 x 8 inches). Drizzle over the reserved pear juice.

Mix together the dry topping ingredients in a large bowl. Pour over the melted butter and combine until the mixture resembles large breadcrumbs. Sprinkle over the fruit and press down firmly.

Place in a preheated oven, 180°C (350°F), Gas Mark 4, for 40–45 minutes or until golden and crisp. Serve with fat-free Greek yogurt, if liked.

For forest fruit & clementine crumble, replace the fresh and dried fruits with 450 g (14 ½ oz) frozen forest fruits, thawed and drained of excess liquid. Slice 2 clementines into segments, discarding the pith, and mix with the forest fruits. Spread the fruit over the base of the ovenproof dish, cover with the crumble topping and bake as above.

very berry & fromage frais fool

Serves **4**

Preparation time **5 minutes**,
  plus cooling and chilling

Cooking time **about
  5 minutes**

3 tablespoons **crème de
  cassis** or **spiced red fruit
  cordial**

250 g (8 oz) **mixed frozen
  berries**

2–4 tablespoons **icing sugar**,
  to taste

500 g (1 lb) **fat-free fromage
  frais**

250 g (8 oz) **low-fat
  blackcurrant yogurt**

1 **vanilla pod**, split in half
  lengthways

toasted **flaked almonds**,
  to serve (optional)

Put the crème de cassis or cordial in a saucepan over a low heat and gently heat, then add the berries. Stir, cover and cook for about 5 minutes or until the fruit has thawed and is beginning to collapse. Remove from the heat and stir in between 1–3 tablespoons of the icing sugar, according to taste. Cool completely, then chill for at least 1 hour.

Mix together the fromage frais, yogurt and 1 tablespoon of the icing sugar in a bowl. Scrape in the seeds from the vanilla pod and beat to combine.

Fold the berries into the fromage frais mixture until just combined. Carefully spoon into decorative glasses or glass serving dishes and serve immediately, scattered with toasted almonds, if liked.

For exotic fruit fool, replace the crème de cassis with 3 tablespoons coconut cream and the mixed berries with 250 g (8 oz) exotic fruit mix and add 1 tablespoon lime juice. Heat as above, then blend in a food processor or blender until smooth. Chill as above. Mix the fromage frais with 2 tablespoons coconut cream and 250 g (8 oz) fat-free mango yogurt instead of the blackcurrant yogurt. Fold in the fruit purée and serve sprinkled with toasted coconut flakes, if liked.

vanilla-spiced fruit salad

Serves **4**
Preparation time **10 minutes**,
  plus cooling
Cooking time **4–5 minutes**

150 ml (¼ pint) **apple juice**
1 **vanilla pod**, split in half
  lengthways
2 tablespoons **agave nectar**
  or **soft light brown sugar**
2 **kiwi fruit**, peeled and sliced
250 g (8 oz) **strawberries**,
  hulled and thickly sliced
125 g (4 oz) **blueberries**
1 **mango**, peeled, stoned
  and sliced
mint leaves, to decorate

Warm the apple juice in a small saucepan with the split vanilla pod and agave nectar or sugar over a medium-low heat. Simmer gently for 4–5 minutes, then leave to cool completely. Remove the vanilla pod and scrape the seeds into the light syrup.

Combine the fruits in a large bowl and drizzle over the vanilla-spiced syrup. Stir gently to coat and spoon into serving bowls. Sprinkle with mint leaves and serve.

For Asian-style fruit salad, replace the apple juice with 150 ml (¼ pint) pineapple juice and simmer in a saucepan with 2 star anise, 1 tablespoon lime juice, 2 cloves and the agave nectar. Leave to cool, then chill for 1 hour. Cut off the top and base of 1 small pineapple and slice off the skin. Cut the pineapple into quarters and remove the core from each quarter. Cut into slices and combine with the mango, a 400 g (13 oz) can drained lychees and 2 sliced star fruits in a serving bowl. Pour over the syrup and serve.

apple & blackberry pie

Serves **4**

Preparation time **20 minutes**, plus chilling

Cooking time **35–40 minutes**

150 g (5 oz) **wholemeal flour**
75 g (3 oz) **plain flour**
125g (4 oz) **chilled butter**
1 tablespoon **caster sugar**
pinch of **salt**
3 **dessert apples**, peeled, cored and sliced
1 teaspoon **lemon juice**
1 teaspoon **almond essence**
1–2 tablespoons **soft dark brown sugar**, to taste (optional)
200 g (7 oz) **fresh** or **frozen blackberries**
2 tablespoons **toasted, chopped almonds** (optional)

Place the flours in a large bowl, add the butter and rub in with the fingertips until the mixture resembles fine breadcrumbs. Stir in the caster sugar and salt. Mix in 3½–4½ tablespoons cold water, adding enough water to form a dough, and knead lightly until smooth. Divide into 2 balls, one slightly larger than the other. Wrap each in clingfilm and chill for 30 minutes.

Put the apples, lemon juice, almond essence and brown sugar in a bowl and toss to coat. Mix in the blackberries and set aside.

Roll out the larger ball of pastry on a lightly floured surface to fit a 23 cm (9 inch) nonstick pie tin. Press the pastry into the tin to come up the sides, moistening the edges with a little cold water. Roll out the smaller ball to fit as a lid. Spoon the fruit evenly over the pastry shell, then scatter over the almonds, if using. Top with the pastry lid, pressing down the dampened edges to seal. Trim away the excess pastry with a sharp knife.

Cut 3 small incisions in the top of the pie and place in a preheated oven, 180°C (350 °F), Gas Mark 4, for 35–40 minutes or until crisp and golden. Leave to rest for 5–10 minutes, then serve in slices with half-fat crème fraîche.

For rhubarb & raspberry pie, replace the dessert apples with 400 g (13 oz) thinly sliced rhubarb and the blackberries with 200 g (7 oz) fresh or frozen raspberries and add the freshly grated rind of 1 lemon. Bake as above until the pastry is crisp and the rhubarb tender. Stir 1 teaspoon rosewater into 4 tablespoons half-fat crème fraîche and serve with the pie.

papaya with tumbling berries

Serves **4**

Preparation time **8 minutes**

2 large **papayas**

125 g (4 oz) **blueberries**

125 g (4 oz) **raspberries**

250 g (8 oz) **strawberries**, sliced

125 g (4 oz) **cherries**, pitted (optional)

runny honey, to taste (optional)

lime wedges, to serve

Cut the papayas in half and scoop out the seeds and discard. Place each half on a serving plate.

Mix together the blueberries, raspberries, strawberries and cherries, if using, in a bowl and then pile into the papaya halves. Drizzle with a little honey, if liked, and serve with the lime wedges.

For papaya & berry smoothie, peel and halve the papayas, remove the seeds and cut into chunks. Place in a food processor or blender with the remaining fruits and 10 ice cubes. Add 500 ml (17 fl oz) apple or guava juice and blend until smooth. Pour into glasses and serve immediately.

balsamic strawberries & mango

Serves **4**

Preparation time **5 minutes**, plus overnight chilling and standing

500 g (1 lb) **strawberries**, thickly sliced

1 large **mango**, peeled, stoned and sliced

1–2 tablespoons **caster sugar**, to taste

3 tablespoons **balsamic vinegar**

2 tablespoons chopped **mint**, to decorate

Mix together the strawberries and mango in a large, shallow bowl, sprinkle with the sugar, according to taste, and pour over the balsamic vinegar. Cover with clingfilm and chill overnight.

Remove the fruit from the refrigerator and leave to stand for at least 1 hour before serving.

Spoon the fruit into serving bowls, drizzle over the syrup and serve, sprinkled with the mint.

For peppery strawberries & blueberries, mix the strawberries with 125 g (4 oz) blueberries and make as above. Sprinkle with a few grinds of black pepper and the chopped mint before serving.

griddled bananas with blueberries

Serves **4**
Preparation time **5 minutes**
Cooking time **8–10 minutes**

4 **bananas**, unpeeled
8 tablespoons **fat-free Greek yogurt**
4 tablespoons **oatmeal** or **fine porridge oats**
125 g (4 oz) **blueberries**
runny honey, to serve

Heat a ridged griddle pan over a medium-hot heat, add the bananas and griddle for 8–10 minutes, or until the skins are beginning to blacken, turning occasionally.

Transfer the bananas to serving dishes and, using a sharp knife, cut open lengthways. Spoon over the yogurt and sprinkle with the oatmeal or oats and blueberries. Serve immediately, drizzled with a little honey.

For oatmeal, ginger & sultana yogurt, mix ½ teaspoon ground ginger with the yogurt in a bowl. Sprinkle with 2–4 tablespoons soft dark brown sugar, according to taste, the oatmeal and 4 tablespoons sultanas. Leave to stand for 5 minutes before serving.

pear, almond & chocolate cake

Serves **4**
Preparation time **10 minutes**
Cooking time **45–50 minutes**

100 ml (3½ fl oz) **groundnut oil**
125 g (4 oz) **fat-free natural yogurt**
1 teaspoon **vanilla extract**
175 g (6 oz) **golden caster sugar**
225 g (7½ oz) **wholemeal flour**
50 g (2 oz) **ground almonds**
2 teaspoons **baking powder**
pinch of **salt**
3 **eggs**, lightly beaten
75 g (3 oz) **plain dark chocolate chips**
1 large firm, ripe **Comice pear**, peeled, cored and coarsely grated
100 g (3½ oz) **whole blanched almonds** (optional)

Beat together the oil, yogurt, vanilla extract, sugar, flour, ground almonds, baking powder and pinch of salt in a large bowl. Add the eggs, one by one, beating well after each addition.

Fold in the chocolate chips and pear and spoon into a deep, round 20 cm (8 inch) nonstick cake tin. Arrange the blanched almonds over the top of the cake, if using.

Place in a preheated oven, 180°C (350°F), Gas Mark 4, for 45–50 minutes or until the cake is risen, golden and firm to the touch.

Leave to cool for 15 minutes in the tin, then remove from the tin and cool completely on a wire rack. Serve in thick wedges with dollops of half-fat crème fraîche, if liked.

For lime & blueberry yogurt cake, make as above, replacing the vanilla extract with the grated rind of 1 lime and the pear with 125 g (4 oz) blueberries. Omit the chocolate chips and blanched almonds. Scatter 2 tablespoons grated coconut over the top before baking. Bake as above.

rice pudding with toasted nuts

Serves **4**
Preparation time **5 minutes**
Cooking time **35–30 minutes**

125 g (4 oz) **brown pudding
    rice**
750 ml (1¼ pints) **skimmed**
    or **semi-skimmed milk**
2 **cardamom pods**, lightly
    crushed
finely grated rind of ½ **lemon**
25 g (1 oz) **soft dark brown
    sugar**, plus extra to serve
    (optional)
1 **vanilla pod**, split in half
    lengthways
100 g (3½ oz) mixed blanched
    nuts, such as **Brazil nuts,
    hazelnuts** and **shelled
    pistachio nuts**

Put the rice in a heavy-based saucepan with the milk,
cardamom, lemon rind and sugar. Scrape in the seeds
from the vanilla pod and place over a medium heat.
Bring to the boil, then reduce the heat, partially
cover and simmer very gently, stirring regularly, for
25–30 minutes, or until the rice is tender and creamy,
adding more milk if necessary.

Meanwhile, place the nuts in a small freezer bag and
tap lightly with a rolling pin until they are crushed but
not ground. Tip into a nonstick frying pan and dry-fry
over a low heat for 5–6 minutes, stirring continuously,
until golden. Tip on to a plate and leave to cool.

Spoon the rice pudding into deep bowls and sprinkle
over a little extra brown sugar, if liked. Scatter over the
toasted nuts and serve immediately.

For fresh fig compote, to serve as an accompaniment,
put 4 roughly chopped fresh figs and 125 ml (4 fl oz)
apple juice in a small pan and simmer gently for
10–12 minutes or until the fruit is tender. Either leave
the compote chunky or blend to a purée in a food
processor or blender.

creamy mango & passion fruit

Serves **4**
Preparation time **10 minutes**

1 large **mango**, peeled, stoned
   and cut into chunks
750 g (1 ½ lb) **fat-free natural
   yogurt**
1–2 tablespoons **agave
   nectar**, to taste
1 **vanilla pod**, split in half
   lengthways
4 **passion fruit**, halved

Place the mango in a food processor or blender and blend to a purée.

Put the yogurt and agave nectar, according to taste, in a large bowl, scrape in the seeds from the vanilla pod and beat together. Gently fold in the mango purée and spoon into tall glasses or glass serving dishes.

Scoop the seeds from the passion fruit and spoon over the mango yogurt. Serve immediately with thin biscuits, if liked.

For blackcurrant & almond yogurt, purée 250 g (8 oz) blackcurrants as above and fold into the yogurt with the agave nectar, according to taste, and 1 teaspoon almond essence. Spoon into tall, glass serving dishes and scatter with toasted almonds, to serve.

mixed berry salad

Serves **4–6**
Preparation time **10 minutes**

400 g (13 oz) **strawberries**
250 g (8 oz) **raspberries**
150 g (5 oz) **blueberries**
150 g (5 oz) **blackberries**
1 small bunch of **mint**, finely
   chopped, a few sprigs
   reserved for decoration
3 tablespoons **elderflower
   syrup**

Hull and halve the strawberries. Wash all the berries and drain well.

Put the berries in a large serving bowl and add the chopped mint and elderflower syrup. Mix together carefully and serve, decorated with the reserved mint sprigs.

For warm berry salad, dilute 100 ml (3½ fl oz) elderflower syrup in 600 ml (1 pint) water, add 50 g (2 oz) caster sugar and bring to the boil in a heavy-based saucepan. Add the berries, prepared as above, to the pan and turn off the heat. Let the berries cool slightly, then serve with half-fat crème fraîche. The berries will keep for up to 5 days in the syrup in the refrigerator.

index

acknowledgements

Executive Editor: Eleanor Maxfield
Managing Editor: Clare Churly
Senior Art Editor: Juliette Norsworthy
Designer: Penny Stock
Photographer: William Shaw
Home Economist: Joy Skipper
Props Stylist: Liz Hippisley
Senior Production Controller: Caroline Alberti

Special photography: © Octopus Publishing Group Limited/William Shaw
Other photography: © Octopus Publishing Group Limited 75, 151; /Stephen Conroy 6, 13, 71, 140, 174, 208; /David Munns 32, 49, 62, 77, 81, 89, 117, 133, 161, 165; /Lis Parsons 14, 25, 65, 98, 109, 113, 121, 127, 139, 153, 169, 201, 203, 205, 233; /William Reavell 97; /William Shaw 69; /Ian Wallace 43, 57, 207.